How Daddy Became A Beachcomber

2014
Happy Beachcombing

by

Marilyn Hedley

Bingy Hedley, Mare's Sis!

Bloomington, IN Milton Keynes, UK

authorHOUSE

AuthorHouse™
1663 Liberty Drive, Suite 200
Bloomington, IN 47403
www.authorhouse.com
Phone: 1-800-839-8640

AuthorHouse™ UK Ltd.
500 Avebury Boulevard
Central Milton Keynes, MK9 2BE
www.authorhouse.co.uk
Phone: 08001974150

First published by AuthorHouse 7/25/2006

ISBN: 1-4259-2811-0 (sc)

Printed in the United States of America
Bloomington, Indiana

This book is printed on acid-free paper.

HOW DADDY BECAME
A BEACHCOMBER

by

MARILYN HEDLEY

ILLUSTRATED BY FLO ANN

CHAPTER 1

When mama decided to write a book about how daddy became a beachcomber, she began to put it off. Mama is the best putter-offer in the world. Daddy swears she put off having me twenty-four hours so she could get her Christmas shopping done. I want to give mama credit for trying, however. All over the house are notebooks on which she has written, "Ideas for book" or "Do not destroy." Inside she has begun, "Beachcombing is an international word. It strikes a responsive chord in the hearts of all men, be they white, yellow, or black" or "You do not have to have seen a beach to be a beachcomber" or "Beachcombing is a state of mind and can be carried on in a rocker on your front porch as well as not." But following these jottings there are a few lines of poetry, a descriptive paragraph about "Cotton Fields in Autumn," or a long unreadable note giving orders to do this and that while she's away; so at a family consultation (without mama) it was decided that I write the book, goodness knows why.

I'm just an ordinary girl of nineteen, who paints a little, writes a little poetry, and as daddy says, "adds to the comfort of everything." I'm the homey one. Of course they don't realize what goes on inside of me. They don't know about the music I hear when I'm watching the sunset, about the purple forests I travel through while a storm is raging across the sea. They'd be too surprised for words where I go sometimes and what I do while I'm bringing in wood for the fireplace, but we won't go into that.

Charlotte Elizabeth, the youngest, is not a child, she's an elf. She was born in Carmel near Point Lobos, which Daddy says is the elves home base. ...So we call Charlotte Elizabeth "The Ba" a name which fits an elf.

When I told mama that I was writing the book, one of those wistful "might have been" shadows crossed her face for a moment, but she rallied quickly and began getting together the "How to

Write" books. Later I hear her tell a friend, "I've started the story at last. Marilyn's writing it."

Bungy, my next to youngest sister, is mama's pet. Mama can't bear to cross her or see her unhappy in any way. The reason for this is because when Bungy was five years old and we didn't have any food, mama took her walking to get her mind off her stomach and right in the midst of a beautiful park with mama pointing out special loveliness like mad, Bungy sat down on the grass, looked up at mama, and said, "I'm hungry."

Mama grabbed her up in her arms and carried her home, dreading to go in because of the empty cupboard. Mama has never forgotten it, but Bungy is a good sport and doesn't take advantage of mama's heart.

Charlotte Elizabeth, the youngest is not a child – she's an elf. Sometimes she's two people, sometimes she's a crowd, and besides she was born in Carmel near Point Lobos which daddy says is the elves' "home base." Every time we go back there, daddy puts his finger to his lips and we tiptoe under the anguished arms of the cypress trees, whose fingers clutch soft, gray-green moss. When we come to the elviest part, we stop and listen. Sure enough, there they are, dancing and singing! As we walk enchanted on the path leading around the point, silent because we can't find words to tell of the beauty of the clear green water and the old gray-green rocks, we can hear their sweet voices.

In trying to describe daddy to an old schoolmate who hadn't met him, mama said, "Oh, he's the type who swears he can hear elves in the trees on Point Lobos, and the worst of it is, the rest of us not only hear them, we see them!"

So we call Charlotte Elizabeth "the Ba." That name better fits an elf.

Sometimes I think it would be better if we didn't have to be so romantic about everything, but I suppose it's more fun this way. Not long ago we were making a bunk room out of an old boat and had to have some big logs for beams in the ceiling. We could have got them anywhere now since we have the money, but no, daddy announced that he would take the saw, hammer, and nails, go up the coast a mile or so, get the logs, make them into a raft, and tow it down to the cove. Flo Ann, my oldest sister, an old salt if I ever saw one, could go along to help with the rowing.

They started early one morning in *Skoal,* our leaky row boat. Their only compromise to the laws governing sea travel was to take our ancient fog horn, which mama uses to call us to dinner. They promised to be back by noon.

Twelve o'clock came, but not daddy and Flo Ann. Three o'clock, six o'clock, and then the sun began to set. Mama, who had been pacing up and down a good deal, drew off by herself to her thinking place. We children realized the seriousness of the situation. Flo Ann had a life-saving badge but she'd never had to save any lives, except those appointed by the gym teacher to drown.

When it seemed as though we couldn't wait any longer we heard the fog horn and saw, silhouetted against the sinking sun, daddy and Flo Ann coming in. Flo Ann was standing in *Skoal,* rowing like mad, her jeans rolled up above her knees, her hair blown by the wind, the "sail on and on" look on her face. Daddy, wearing only shorts and a straw hat perched over one ear, was on the crazily swinging raft, shouting like a drunken sailor. His loot was piled high about him. Such starfishes, such lovely shells! He even had a baby octopus. The tide was full, so they had no trouble nosing the little boat and raft into safe harbor.

That night as we sat toasting marshmallows around the fireplace, mama murmured something about it being too bad her heart's blood had to go into the making of a mere bunk room, but daddy laughed and kissed her and the "heavenly satisfaction look" came over her face, and all was well.

CHAPTER 2

This cove where we live is magic, a bit of heaven between a high hill and the sea. It's shaped like a new moon with White Point at one end and Portuguese Bend at the other, a mile of gray, pebbly beach in between. An hour's drive from Hollywood, it seems out of this world.

Long, long ago, the King of Spain gave an early settler acres of land along the sea. This Spanish caballero searched the coast for a place sheltered from the wind and storms and found our cove. He here planted palm trees, Brazilian peppers, Copa de Oro vines, and geraniums, every color under the sun. A little stream falling down the mountain and flowing through the center of the land watered the plants. Here he built huge rock fireplaces, and barbecue pits, using fossilized rocks from the beach. Here he built his hacienda, which by the time we had found it had shrunk to a tiny shack and a few tool houses.

From the high front gate to our house is an eighth of a mile. Our shop is farther up the beach, and the pelicans stand on the steps. Daddy revels in this atmosphere and dreams up driftwood tables, lamps, and chairs while the moon makes a silver path on the waters and marks the white hills with mysterious shadows.

Some days we tramp along the sea for miles to Abalone Cove and on to Point Vicente, picking up anything we think daddy might use, mostly driftwood, but even old shoes – artistic old shoes, green with age and barnacles on the toes. When the lights come on in both lighthouses, the one to the east and the one to the west, we build a big fire, cook our supper, and afterward trudge home to the music of the sea and the whisper of the wind.

Daddy says the cove is an experience, not a place at all. To prove his point, he cites the example of a business man who came down tired and noisy and left refreshed and quiet. The man blustered in, intent on buying some of our screw-ballish patio stuff made from driftwood and getting away as quickly as possible. Bungy and The

Our shop is further up the beach, and pelicans stand at the door. Daddy revels in this atmosphere and dreams up driftwood tables, lamps and chairs.

Ba opened the gate for him. The led him first to the big fireplace by the two Royal Palms. A driftwood fire was burning, rainbow colored, and the sea was singing a gurgling song as it played with the rocks on the shore. Birds flitted and chirped in the interlocked branches of the trees overhead and one lit on the cobblestones at his feet. Bungy and The Ba left him standing very still looking out to sea where a huge freighter was slipping silently by. When daddy came down with the catalogue and order book, the business man acted as if he was in a dream – a very young and happy dream. He said, "I know this is a funny request, but may I stay a while, an hour or so? Can I go beachcombing?"

He was on the plump side so we couldn't find any jeans to fit him. We rolled his trousers up above his knees and found him an old sweater. Off he went up the beach to see what he could find. When he came back, he had a seaweed crown on his head, a string of corks over his shoulders, and his arms and pockets were full of small shells and abalone coral. He was as thrilled as we are when we find Easter eggs. He even had some new things figured out for daddy to make. After that, he came often and took up painting with water colors.

Mama says she has the strangest feeling about our house. Either it is the worst thing in the world or else it is what she has always wanted. Of course, necessities for a perfect home are very few, she says. Loving arms to hold you close, a walk in the moonlight after dinner, laughter at table, and candlelight. The house anyone lives in doesn't have much to do with his home. This one we live in wouldn't suit anyone but us. It's nice, though, living in a house we know we couldn't sell for love nor money. It's ours!

We go at anything exactly the opposite of what people say we should. Most all housebuilders put in urgent things first and leave the decorating to the last, but not us! Consequently, we are still without a few urgent things like roofs that don't leak, cement around stove pipes, and a television set. What we do have, however, is a beautiful rope fence, an oar gate, and a boat door.

We had to make the cellar doors in the front hall because our friend Jack Norworth (you know, "Shine on Harvest Moon" and "Take Me Out To the Ball Game") gave us a huge old cellar key. One thing led to another. If cellar doors, why not a cellar? We

9

wonder now how we could have thought of not having one. It's little, but with a cobwebby red light and lined with big rocks, it's spooky enough for any of us when we have to go in for potatoes or onions. Daddy says any child who has not experienced going to the cellar on a dark winter's night for an orange or an apple is likely to grow up without a soul.

Our dining deck is a bit unhandy since the kitchen is downstairs, but when we're all around the long table, sitting on the barrel chairs with ship's wheel backs, the candelabra burning softly, who cares? The feeling that perhaps we should have been more practical which stole over us, as we carried the last big platter upstairs, is forgotten.

Mama confided in me that all through her life, even when she was a little girl, she had a vision. It was of herself leaning from an open window, the sea beyond, a climbing pink rose beneath, and a pigeon flying overhead. Daddy says a sea gull is as good as a pigeon any day. At last mama has her pigeon vision.

CHAPTER 3

We haven't always lived here. In fact, we've only been in California twelve years, I think. There's no use asking mama, she wouldn't know. She got so mixed up about our ages, heights, and weights during rationing application that it took her months to get everything cleared up. Daddy swears we've been here only ten years; then he looks at Charlotte Elizabeth, who is eleven and born soon after we came to California, and can't figure it out.

We children, all except The Ba, started in Seminole, Oklahoma, where Daddy had three Piggly Wiggly grocery stores. Our house there was built by Eli and Malcolm while they were romancing and moved into by Mr. and Mrs. Eli Hedley. Eli and Malcolm were madly in love. Still are. Sometimes they embarrass us. It's like watching the movies. Mama admits that ever since daddy kissed her under the water tower and proposed in the bakery, she's been putty in his hands. The proposal in the bakery was unique. Mama was teaching school and daddy had put in his first grocery store in Seminole. Daddy and mama had been out of town to a dance. About a mile from home they ran out of gas. On their walk back they passed Mr. Spiegal's bakery. The temperature outside was about 20° above zero. They went inside to rest. They sat in front of the big ovens, warming their feet and munching hot loaves of bread.

Suddenly daddy said, "Gosh, this bread is good. Can you make bread?"

"No," mama confessed.

"Then we'll buy our bread here," fairly shouted daddy, warming up to his subject. He grabbed her by the hands, drew her up from the chair, and yelled, "Yes, darling, we will, won't we? Together we'll buy our bread here the rest of our lives," while all the bakers looked on delighted.

Daddy told us about their wedding night also. Mama was born in Oklahoma and daddy lived there many years, so both of them had thousands of friends. They were married in February; because they were so much in love, they couldn't wait until mama's school was out. Mr. Kitchens, the school superintendent, gave mama one week off for a honeymoon. They couldn't go far in a week, so daddy engaged a suite a the Skirvin Hotel in Oklahoma City, and directly following the wedding at five o'clock in the afternoon they rushed to the hotel, about an hour's drive from Seminole. Upon their arrival, mama got as lovely as she could in her satin housecoat, daddy as man of the hour-ish as he could in his red wood smoking jacket with satin lapels.

The dinner daddy ordered sent up, was sent up. The fire burned softly in the fireplace. The stage was set for a perfect "first night" … then friends began to arrive! Good old friends that had followed them and were now paying calls. All night long, they came. It was touching to see how happy they felt their calls would make the newly-weds, as they drew bottles of champagne from under their coats. Morning came and there was nothing for daddy to do but order breakfast for everyone. At ten o'clock daddy pushed the last friend out of the door and he and mama, with heavy eyelids, fell into exhausted sleep.

Flo came first, I followed soon after, then there were five years during which time we had a fire, remodeled the house, and planted a jungle. Indirectly the fire was black Carrie's fault. Had she not gathered us around her knees and read us her version of Robinson Crusoe, we would not have had to find the desert isle and build the fire. Her version! Carrie had finished the eighth grade in the colored school but reading lines as they were written was much too tedious and boring for her.

Flo Ann and I chose Lou Ann and Janet Lancaster, our best friends, to be our companions in adventure. We set sail, cracking up immediately in the attic. What a place to be shipwrecked! Old blankets to lie on; all sorts of odds and ends to stoke our fire with. The food problem was yet unsolved, however, so we had to leave camp to forage. Leaving the fire burning brightly, we stole carefully down the steps and out the kitchen door, searching among the blackberry vines in the garden for ripe berries.

I'll never forget Carrie the way we saw her next. She was standing at the foot of the ladder stairs, the smoke billowing out all around her, her eyes rolling ceilingward, her hands flying up and down, murmuring softly, "Oh, Lawd! Oh, Lawd! Do something!"

Carrie was on good terms with "De Lawd." He never failed her. This time the telephone rang. A friend of ours wanted to know when mama and daddy would be back from Oklahoma City. Carrie gave the alarm to her and soon the firemen dashed up in the fire engine. They started shooting water everywhere, moving furniture out in the yard, and making glorious bedlam. What a day! Everyone was talking about where we'd stay that night. Friends were making ready guest rooms. We had lunch at one place and tea another; then were taken back to our beautifully wrecked house to await shiveringly the coming of mama and daddy. Every time we looked at Carrie we wanted to cry, she was so mournful.

They had all reckoned, however, without our parents. Arriving at dusk and sizing up the situation, daddy gave a big belly laugh, gathered us up in his arms, began dancing around the living room floor among the debris and sang out to Carrie, "Polly put the kettle on! We'll all have tea." Mama was laughing and crying at the same time, going around picking up her broken treasures and throwing them in the wastebasket. Carrie flew into action. She made a big fire in the fireplace and put the kettle on. The neighbors shook their heads and I heard one of them say, "I suppose it's the relief of finding the children safe that makes them act that way." But I don't know, I caught the look in daddy's eye when he announced, "We'll camp here in the back bedroom" – the same kind of look he has when the whole family is gathered around the table, the fire is burning brightly, the sea is pounding mightily, and the rain is tapping shyly on the dormer window. Daddy can never resist an adventure, even it it's only a camping trip in the back bedroom.

CHAPTER 4

Then was when we began to suspect that daddy had ideas. Such dreams went into the remodeling of the burnt house! A huge nursery on top, another fireplace, an extra bathroom made the house more fun than ever; and because he used so many ideas, there was some insurance money left over. Mama never had a cent because she always spent her allowance as soon as she got it, so she was sparkly-eyed when daddy gave her the money with a fine presentation speech, saying solemnly, "This is yours with no strings attached." As though there were ever any strings on money mama got her hands on.

Daddy thought mama would buy something for herself or the house, but he figured without mama's imagination. The next week, while he was away in Chicago attending a Rotary convention, an old man called at the house selling plants and trees. Either it was his cute little white goatee or the word picture he painted of how tropical the yard would look filed with Chinese this and that which caused mama to use the insurance money for part of her order and resort to the installment plan for the rest.

When daddy came home, the garden was planted so densely with huge shrubs that he could hardly find the house. Mama hastened to explain that although it might be unhandy pushing our way to the front door, still the trees were picturesque. That is always the perfect answer to daddy. Consider not at all inconvenience, consider not cost, consider only beauty. So mama kissed daddy and the "heavenly satisfaction look" came over his face, and all was well. He stood in deep thought for a moment, then shouted, "Lige, bring the ladder and some pipes."

15

Soon after, old Lige, our gardener, and daddy were scrambling around all over the roof placing pipes with holes drilled in them, and that's how our raining system was born. They joined a quarter inch pipe onto our water line and ran it up the side of the house, behind a trellis of vines, along the peak of the roof, in all directions. Every few yards they placed an old-fashioned circulating sprinkler. They arranged to turn it off and on from our screened back porch. After that, friends lifted eyebrows, but we children scampered to do it, when daddy called, "Go turn on the rain." As daddy said, "What's the use of having a jungle if we can't have a tropical storm?" So, during the dry, hot season, we had cooling rain pattering on the roof and dripping through the vines and into the flower beds at the windows. As far as we knew ours was the only raining device in Oklahoma, or in the world for that matter. However, since coming to California, we find one at Don Beachcomber's in Hollywood, but what we can't figure out is whether he copied us or we copied him.

Early in November of that year, came a little sister … When we finally got over the disappointment of the expected brother being a girl and had decided to call her Bungy, short for Bungy Rabbit, which Carrie had called her from the minute she was born, it was the day before Christmas. All day people had been coming and going, mama uttering little squeals of delight. In the kitchen Carrie reigned supreme. Some "cousins" were helping her and all sorts of good things kept popping out of the oven. Carrie was singing most of the day, stopping only long enough to shout "Christmas gift" to any of mama's friends whose noses had led the way to the kitchen, or to finger wistfully a silver ring made and sent to her by Cody, the father of her five children, serving sentence in the Oklahoma penitentiary at McAlester. The house was all bubbly with suspenseful confusion. The gifts kept piling higher and higher under the tree. Evening drew on into night. Snow was falling and we children were being made ready for bed. "There'll be enough for a snow man tomorrow," we shouted as we scampered around the nursery. Finally Carrie tucked us in and the gay hubbub downstairs became a faint murmur to our sleepy ears. Our nurse stood at the window and looked out at the pretty red and green pattern the tree lights made on the snow. I wonder if she was thinking of her own little brood waiting for Santa Claus in the dark, smoky house across the tracks.

Mr. H. W. McNeil was our friend and a character. Every Christmas he started celebrating. He'd turn himself out like a bandbox – spats, derby, white gloves and cane. He'd stuff his pockets full of bills. He'd load "Mink," his colored boy, with bottles of "Scotch" and off they'd go, distributing money and drinks to the poor people, ending up at our house for the Christmas breakfast daddy always gave for his pals.

Afterwards the real fun started when Mr. McNeil delivered groceries to the poorer, poor people. That Christmas Flo, mama, daddy, and I went with him. We drove off in Mr. McNeil's old-fashioned, three-seated Packard. It had a little folding seat in the middle. Mink drove and daddy sat in front with him. Flo, mama, and I were on the back seat, while our host, straight and dignified, occupied the middle one.

We came to an alley with a row of pigpens, having roofs of a sort. Mink stopped the car. Mr. McNeil got out and made his way a little unsteadily across the snow. He knocked on a tin door. There was no answer. As he began to pull the door open a pink snout appeared, followed by the body and tail of a pig. It shot between Mr. McNeil's legs, almost upsetting him. He looked nonplussed for a moment, waved his hand toward us in the car, turned and swept his derby gallantly to he ground in the direction of the fleeing pig. "Madame, I beg your pardon," he said. We almost died laughing. "This is a real pig-pen," he shouted. Come help me find Mary's pen."

We climbed from the car and followed him to the next hut. Again he knocked. This time the door was pushed open by a frowsy woman with a thin, dirty face. "Hello, Mary," said Mr. McNeil, "can we come in?"

"Ah, it's you, sir," she answered as we squeezed through the narrow opening into the black little room. As our eyes got accustomed to the darkness, we began to see things. Under heaps of dirty blankets were children. On the dirt floor, a camp fire was smoldering. Off to one side was a skillet filled with pasty gravy. It was awfully cold in there. Mink brought in the big box. The children sprang from their corners, fell on their knees around it, and began to tear it open. Mary did too, but she was crying. A dirty coal oil lamp on a shelf cast its faint rays directly upon them. "Look, mama," whispered Flo Ann, "they look like a praying Christmas card." Mr. McNeil took a monogrammed, white linen handkerchief from his pocket and blew his nose, hard.

That afternoon we made a snow man, put one of mama's old hats on its head, a fur boa around its neck, and called it Mary.

CHAPTER 5

For some time we children had heard the word Depression. Mama's and daddy's friends must have enjoyed talking about it or they wouldn't have so often. Never let it be said, however, that our parents acted in any way according to specifications. As people began to spend less money, they began to spend more till finally Uncle Tom told daddy he was making "one of those things" out of himself by insisting on keeping all of his clerks employed at the stores; and on their same salaries. About this time daddy thought to recoup his finances and balance the no-customer hole, by investing in Monarch Lead of Arizona. When that company's New York representative called him from the Big City and said over the telephone, "Hedley, if you were my own brother, I'd tell you to mortgage everything and invest as much as you can in Monarch Lead," daddy did just that. We got beautiful, most encouraging letters from that company right up to the time they declared bankruptcy.

That summer in Oklahoma was very dry. Our raining system was turned on most of the time. More and more often friends came by for a little relief from the heat, and as I look back on it now, I feel to be comforted by mama's and daddy's lack of respect for the Depression.

One day, Carrie asked mama for the afternoon off. She wanted to join some other "Sistahs and Brothas" in Colored Town to pray for rain. We went in the car with mama to take her across the tracks to the little church. Wewoka Avenue was blistering hot and dusty.

Through the double doors, open to any wandering breeze, we saw kneeling figures and heard their soft chanting voices asking "De Lawd" to send rain. That night when we were having watermelon in the garden, big drops of water fell on our faces and everybody went wild with joy.

The first week in July, daddy closed out the third and last store and sold our house. It was very sad because after he paid off the mortgage we didn't have much money left. The stores, with their empty shelves, looked bleak and lonely, and daddy's eyes were filled with unfulfilled dreams. We knew we were going somewhere, but we didn't know where. Mama wanted to go West but she wanted to go East before she went West. She hadn't forgotten those lovely antiques she had picked up on her last vacation in Asheville, North Carolina.

For the one and only time in his life daddy turned practical. "No," he said, "We'll go West. We're more familiar with the country. We know a few people, and besides we won't need so many clothes."

So the last week in July, with a mighty big tug on roots and a tearful goodbye to friends, house, jungle, raining system, and Carrie, mama, daddy, Flo, Bungy, and I drove into the sunset. We took with us, besides our baggage, a few books, our Christmas tree decorations, and a huge cuckoo clock, which the Rotary Club had appropriately given daddy as a "going away" gift.

The first few days out, we were sad and didn't find much to interest us; still, daddy had mama and mama had daddy, Flo had me and I had Flo, and Bungy had her "corner." We had begged her to throw the blanket, which held the ragged dirty end away but she couldn't do it. The nose-rubbing corner was a sight, but when cuddly Bungy rubbed her nose and her lovely big eyes got sleepy and soft, she looked so happy nobody had the courage to deprive her of it. So it was not until we passed Salt Lake City and saw Bungy tear off her precious corner and hurl it out of the window that we began to wake up and realize that there had been a change.

We never see the things we're supposed to see on a trip, but we certainly see a lot of others. Like the old man who lived on a hill in a little hut all by himself and was happy as a lark writing poetry instead of keeping accounts which he had done for years; like the junk man who showed us a Wells Fargo money chest. He had lived with the flies so long that he carried on a conversation with them on the side snorting and sniffing.

He showed us around his place as though he were the host and his junk pile a fine estate. He was tall and graceful and his gray hair hung almost to his shoulders. He used good grammar except when he talked to the flies, then he said anything. Ever so often he stopped in the middle of a long dissertation, struck out wildly with his arms, turned his head to one side, began snorting, and said, "Gee Dee you flies! I thought I told you to go home." After each battle, he picked up his conversation where he had dropped it as though nothing had happened.

Every once in a while on the trip, mama's conscience stirred feebly and she said something about maybe we should get settled because, after all, we *were* expecting a little brother, and so at last we came to Monterey.

CHAPTER 6

Monterey: color, history, crisp golden air of Autumn the whole year through, and as mama said, not a town at all – only a mood. She found it much too exciting for baby-having, so peaceful Carmel was chosen to be the expected baby brother's birthplace.

Mama and daddy had never in their married experience rented a house; consequently they had all kinds of fears when they approached Mr. Janes, the sculptor, seeking his cottage, North Light, which they had seen advertised in the *Carmel Pine Cones* "For Rent" column. With three children and mama giving every indication of another one in the offing, they didn't feel as though their chances were too good. To their surprise and delight Mr. Janes consented to us as tenants quite readily. Later when mama said, "How could you make up your mind so quickly, us with children and all?" he answered, "Oh, I consider children one of the necessary evils."

Sparkling blue water, fragrance of burning eucalyptus logs, and the barking of seals make Oklahoma seem farther away than ever. Carmel is full of quaint people and fleas; however, the fleas soon become a habit and you hardly notice them at all. Everybody in Carmel scratches – some furtively, others openly. Few are quite as noisy about it as our poet friend who sold real estate as a side line or vice versa, and who wore a stiff bosom shirt with celluloid collar and cuffs. Flowery conversation flowed in a constant stream from his lips. Sometimes he became excited and this always affected the fleas. He scratched energetically here and there! He made his stiff shirtfront, collar, and cuffs pop, daddy said, like "popcorn on a hot stove in winter."

Instead of a brother, The Elf put in her appearance in late August, and there followed four lovely months. As the money began to dwindle, it dawned upon daddy that some people have to work for a living and he was probably one of them, so we tugged gently (up came very light roots), said goodbye to North Light, our house, eucalyptus fragrance, and barking seals, and made for Hollywood.

We arrived in Hollywood one night in December about a week before Christmas. Santa Claus Lane (nee Hollywood Boulevard) was ablaze with lights. Huge red and white tin Christmas trees camouflaged the lampposts. Twinkling stars amidst garlands of green formed an arch running from one side of the street to the other.

From around the corner on Vine Street came Santa Claus. His workshop was mounted on the most beautiful sleigh in the world, pulled by eight sparkling white reindeer. From within the quaint house came soft music, - "Silent Night, Holy Night." Snow swirled over the mechanical dwarfs busily making toys, and Santa Claus, with a lovely movie actress at his side, called out merrily to us all, "Happy Christmas, little girls and boys." Our hearts stood still. Never, never had we seen anything so wonderful.

Now that I am older I have moments of thinking Christmas is too commercial but always when I stand on Hollywood Boulevard at 7:30 on a December evening and Santa Claus drives down the "lane," I forget the palm trees, the tawdry glitter of the shop windows, the unhappy faces of the swarms of unhappy people, and remember only the beautiful shiny side of it.

After the parade we found a tourist court out on Ventura Boulevard in the San Fernando Valley. Ours didn't look as nice as some of the others we passed. A fat woman with three children hanging on to her skirts peered at us from an open doorway as we moved in.

Mama looked embarrassed and daddy hurried with our baggage and the antique cradle which held our precious Ba. He waited until the fat woman had closed her door and started rattling pots and pans before he brought in the cuckoo clock, the books, the Christmas tree decorations, and the sleigh bells. These last, daddy had nostalgically purchased at Noah's Ark in Pacific Grove when we still had some money. None of us could get to sleep that night.

CHAPTER 7

'T was the day before Christmas and not snowing. The California sun was working hard for the Chamber of Commerce. It all seemed unreal and we children were heavy-hearted. A few packages had come through the mail, mama and daddy had sneaked a few in under their coats, but nothing was the same as we remembered it. Mama's eyes were red and her laughs ended suddenly as she turned her back to us.

At darkness, a miracle occurred. The fog began to come in. A soft mistiness covered the trees and earth.

"By Jove," daddy shouted, "we're going out to get a tree."

"That's it," mama said, "a tree. Ba and I will stay here and dust the decorations, and pop some popcorn for stringing."

Flo, Bungy, daddy, and I marched out jingling sleigh bells and singing, "Deck the halls with boughs of holly." As we drove around from tree lot to tree lot and saw the prices on the trees, daddy didn't sing quite so much. Then the places began to close. After all, business was over for that year as everyone had already got a tree. Everyone almost. It began to mist harder and harder. We were driving down Wilshire on what seemed by now to be a hopeless quest, when suddenly out of the darkness, we saw scattered on the ground, big boughs of evergreen. White and green wreaths with bright satin bows lay everywhere. A dealer had abandoned his work, taken down his tent, and gone home for the season. "This is it!" daddy shouted and stopped the car. Out we jumped, laughing and dancing, and began picking up the lovely, dewy sprigs of green.

"No whole trees, but we can make a beauty by wiring these moist fragrant branches together," said daddy, laughing.

We filled the car to overflowing and hurried home in high glee to mama and Ba. We put hundreds of wreaths around our necks, filled our arms with evergreens, and burst joyfully in the front door. "Merry Christmas, mama, Merry Christmas, Ba!" we shouted. Soon the living-bedroom was transformed – wreaths fit for a castle hung everywhere. In the window, the tree looked happy and glowing. We drank each other's health with the ever-present hot chocolate. The "heavenly satisfaction look" was on mama's face.

Daddy said, "I'd give anything to hear our landlady in the morning when she spots that wreath on her front door. She'll say, "Who in the hell put this thing here?"

Mama said, "I wonder if Cody sent Carrie a silver ring again this year?"

CHAPTER 8

And so with everyone in California making money on open-air fruit stands, daddy decided to put in a closed one. In fact, it was going to be a little more than closed; it was going to be practically sealed. Daddy had an idea. It was to be christened the Fruit Cellar.

We sold our car to get the money needed to start this project. The first big problem was to rent the spot on Ventura Boulevard which daddy wanted with all his heart. It was owned by Mr. Weddington, North Hollywood Bank president. Everyone said he'd never let daddy have it for such an unorthodox thing as a cellar.

Daddy was getting shabby around the cuffs and it took all the courage he could muster to go into the bank and call for the president. Our daddy has a quiet air of authority which came in handy more than once to cover his threadbareness, and it worked now.

He was admitted immediately. His heart sank when he saw Mr. Weddington. Surely a man without an imagination. Surely a man whose blood had turned to figures. Daddy simply blurted it out – could he have the land on Ventura Boulevard above Whitsett to dig a cellar and fix it up for selling fruits and vegetables? The cool dampness would keep apples and potatoes much fresher and crispier -!

Mr. Weddington looked amazed for a moment, got down behind his desk, and came up with a cute little painted barrel. He said, "Have an apple, Hedley." After thirty minutes of happy apple munching and nostalgic reminiscences of Autumn, apples, maples, and cellars, daddy left, having rented the land from Mr. Weddington for fifteen dollars a month.

We began to dig. How we dug – until at last we could pour the cement. When this hardened, we were ready to make the peaked roof. The shingles for this were made from apple box boards, aged in a vinegar and rusty nails concoction.

Then came the decorating. An old cart was put outside overflowing with pumpkins, squashes, and California holly. The floor was covered with sawdust, old lanterns were hung from the ceiling, and gaily painted barrels placed along the side for oranges, tangerines, nectarines, and walnuts. We found a dead apple tree in a field, sprayed it white, put it in the corner and tied apples and suckers on it. These were to be used as favors on opening day.

Hugh Herbert, the movie actor and Mayor of Studio City, said in his newspaper column about it, "Did you notice that peculiar house on Ventura near Whitsett. Deep set? I wondered what it was for, but now I know. It is a vegetable and fruit cellar to be opened by Hedley … and he claims that vegetables and fruits kept that way will retain their freshness longer, also hold their flavor. He is going to try and have every vegetable. … Good luck. Woo-woo-"

He wrote this in the *Studio City News* a few days before we opened, and we thought it was awfully nice of him. We liked the candy bars he gave all of us children, too.

One morning when we came down, the handsomest cowboy we ever saw was sitting on the thick cellar doors polishing his gun – a beautiful blonde in a sunbonnet and a gingham apron was leaning on the cart. A movie company was shooting a Western. Daddy had high hopes!

The night before opening day, it began to rain. We had a Model-A Ford truck for bringing vegetables from the big wholesale market on Seventh Street. Mama couldn't think of letting daddy go alone to get the stock so she went with him. They started at five o'clock in the morning, got to the market, loaded the truck with colorful lusciousness, and came sailing back to the valley across Laurel Canyon – when, boom, they had a flat tire right in front of a big house. Mama told us a family was having breakfast around a table set in the window overlooking the road. Each person stared without smiling. Mama thought she and daddy must look awfully funny. The rain poured in sheets. Daddy never has any tools where he can get his hands on them so he was dragging them out of here and there all over the car. He had a jack, but wouldn't work, so he had to go off down the road and hunt for a rock to put under the wheel to hold it up.

Then there was the problem of getting the wheel onto the rock. He pulled an old fence post across the road for that.

While daddy was rummaging around in the rain, getting wetter all the time, looking for all the world like Southwest Wind Esquire in *King of the Golden River,* mama was sitting in the little open truck with the family's stares upon her. She squirmed, arranged the blanket over her knees, fooled with her hair, dried the water off her face, and couldn't laugh as much as she wanted to because of the lump in her throat.

She and daddy thought of the white house in Seminole, of Carrie and Lige, and of how good a cup of coffee would taste.

Mama and Daddy thought of the white house in Oklahoma and of how a good cup of coffee would taste.

When they arrived in Studio City, they could hardly see the fruit cellar for rain. They jumped from the car, ran up the cobblestone walk, which we children helped to make, threw open the cellar doors, started down the steps and stopped! Yes, sure enough, it was half full of water! After the first shock daddy's idea factory began to function again and he talked seriously of getting a boat and selling from it, but mama put her foot down. He'd have to wait, like Noah, until the waters subsided. That was the time we had the floods in California. It rained without stopping for a week. The cellar got fuller and fuller. Our venture ended before it started. That's why we children can't eat cauliflower, squash, or rutabaga now – we had to eat the Fruit Cellar.

CHAPTER 9

The tourist court got smaller and smaller and harder and harder to bear. Daddy worked here and there, but never for long, and the look on his face was worse than not having any money.

We children peeked through our doors one night and heard mama and daddy quarreling. "We might as well go back to Seminole," said mama. "It wasn't half as mediocre as this environment."

"All right!" shouted daddy. "You wanted to come as badly as I did. Don't you have any backbone?"

"Plenty!" mama retorted. "Anyhow, enough to get out of this stuffy rut we're in."

They glared furiously at each other across the room for moment – then mama's shoulders slumped and she looked as if she was going to cry. Daddy sprang across to her, gathered her in his arms, and whispered, "You're right darling, I've been afraid – now, I'm not. We'll clear out of here tomorrow morning and find a place more befitting the Hedleys." The "heavenly satisfaction look" was on mama's face as they crawled into bed.

The next morning off we went, taking with us even nice memories of our life there. Mama says laughingly that she dares not stop longer than two hours with all of us or she begins to pick up precious memories to carry around with her. Mama is an incurable sentimentalist.

We big children rode in the back of the truck, covered with slightly frayed blankets. Daddy, mama, and The Ba rode in front. It was a most joyous ride, the cool wind in our faces, the sun beaming down to warm us. We took the road along the sea through Palos Verdes. At Point Vicente the fog set in. So mysterious and quiet. Such soft grayness everywhere.

Daddy shouted back to us, "We need rose-colored spectacles to find a home in this soup, you know." We laughed at daddy's little joke and couldn't have been happier. As we rounded the hill that circles White Point the fog lifted like a curtain going up on a stage, to show us a shimmering expanse of blue water, white sails in the distance, and delicately etched Catalina Island as a backdrop – and there, right before our eyes, standing out like a house seen through a kaleidoscope, we saw it. Perched recklessly on the edge of a 250-foot cliff, without windowpanes or doors, it somehow managed to look dignified.

Daddy stopped the car in front of the locked wooden gate and we walked into the patio over the broken-down wooden fence. An outdoor faucet dripped water. Little birds twittered and drank. Fig trees held ripe, black fruit. But the house inside was a picture of desolation. Holes in the floor and roof, paper hanging from the walls, the only bright spot, a dirty brick fireplace with bricks falling out of it – but oh, the view! At every window was a magnificent panorama of sea and sky. Lords of heaven and earth we'd be in this little ramshackle house. We had to have it! On the leeward side, we found a sign giving the owner's telephone number. Only the gulls and pelicans flying past could possibly have seen it. Like a madman, daddy rushed out to reach him. We stayed and ate figs.

When daddy came back, we moved in. That night we slept in front of the fire, Ba in her antique cradle, mama on her fur coat she'd brought from Oklahoma, and the rest of us on palm leaves covered with blankets. High in the heavens, the moon shone aristocratically. Far below, the surf played a symphony. At last, we were in a house befitting the Hedleys.

CHAPTER 10

Early the next morning we crept down the sides of the cliff on a worn out path to the sea below and entered a new world. It was as though the sea was our good, good friend; a mother, maybe. To this day we always speak of her as she.

On the blue water, diamonds danced and sparkled in the path of the rising sun. A little black sea lion looked at us innocently and slid into his tide pool. Mama found a rock hewn by the waves to resemble a throne. We christened it "The Queen's Seat." All of us took turns sitting in it, the waves splashing around us, the wind in our faces, the salt spray on our lips. It felt and tasted so good after the tourist court.

And the driftwood; what can I say of it? It's been everything to us! Food, clothing, furniture, beauty, and warmth; but that morning it filled us with speechless delight. Daddy began to gather huge flat boards; mama, the round white walking stick pieces; and we children the doll pieces we could use for our puppet show.

Beautiful blue and green abalone shell lay everywhere half full of the receding tide. "Like bowls of soup," mama said. "Bowls of soup," echoed daddy. "Why not? 'Twill be only a matter of stopping up the holes along the back." Eagerly, we began to collect them.

Over a black rock was stretched a rich colored brown net. On one side of it ran a lead line for weighting. "Just the thing for stopping these hoses in the abalones," shouted daddy. "We'll melt the lead and pour it while it's hot."

We love the sea very much but never more than we did that first morning. It was as though time had stopped; that little stretch of beach was the world, and we were safe, forever. It was not until there was a pink glow everywhere and the moon had hung out a bright star that we heard the little house calling.

We slowly climbed the hill. Mama carried Ba, daddy the driftwood, and we children the abalone shells, corks, and fish net. All of us carried dreams in our hearts.

And the driftwood, what can I say of it? It's been everything to us. Food, clothing, furniture.

By the end of the week we had "Little House" putting its arms around us when we came in from a hard day's beachcombing. Two old portholes, found the second day, made charming front windows. Fish net, caught up with old brown rope and corks hung where it softened the walls. A woven driftwood door partly hid the kitchen.

The dining room was the best, though. The table was built on a heavy wine barrel. Thick driftwood boards, hewn and sandpapered until they shone, made the top. Barrels were used for corner cupboards. The holes in the abalones were stopped, and daddy mounted them on corks to they'd sit straight and have oomph. We used them for everything, soup, breakfast food, crackers, popcorn, and candleholders. We hewed plates from pieces of a driftwood log and carved our names on six of them. We put Friend 1, Friend 2, etc. on extra ones. Glasses and cups worried us for a while, but when daddy began to pour over a little book called "Glass Cutting at Home" and to get that certain look in his eye we knew something was about to happen and hoped it was glasses and cups. The day came. He used the kerosene string method to cut ginger ale bottles or any kind we could get. The Japanese Saki was the loveliest. A color blue, as deep as the sea and as soft as the sky. To cut a bottle you saturate an ordinary cotton twine string with coal oil. Tie it around the bottle at the place you want to cut it. Then strike a match and light the end of the string. At the height of its heat, while it is burning merrily, trickle a few drops of cold water above the string, letting it run down the glass to it. You'll hear a "plink" and off comes the top of the bottle. He smoothed the glasses around the top by rubbing them on sandstone.

The table looked so pretty when it was ready for dinner. The fishnet cloth made the top shine more than ever. Candlelight brought out soft pinks in the blue shell bowls. The glasses were forever merry even when they were empty. We hadn't learned about how delicious abalone chowder is or how good California lobster, so we ate potato soup and hot biscuits mainly. We children loved these and caused mama and daddy to laugh heartily one evening when we asked, "Why don't we eat potato soup and hot biscuits when we have money? They're our favorites."

Daddy used the kerosene string method. Japanese Saki bottles were the lovliest. A color as deep as the sea and as soft as the sky.

In turn they caused us to laugh when they demonstrated the bundling bed. Daddy fixed it the way it was so it could be used for a couch. He built a driftwood frame over and down the middle. It could be leaned back upon both ways. One night daddy crawled in on one side of the fence, mama on the other, and they pretended to go to sleep.

"But ah," punned daddy, after snoring loudly a while, "here's the catch!" He sat up, pulled the lever, and the partition which separated them shot up to the ceiling. Now he could snuggle with mama as much as he wanted to and proceeded to do just that. How we giggled!

"Little house" made us happy all right, but it couldn't make us clean without a bathroom. We all agreed the ritual of the tin tub made a good *Saturday Evening Post* cover but that was the only good thing about it. Daddy began scuttling about with that look in his eye. After all, we were 250 feet above the sea. Anything could happen to "let out" bath water if it could run from a pipe extending over the cliff. Besides, a little water would taste good to the nasturtiums which tossed themselves flamingly over the hillside. After the tub room was built, we kept cleaner because it turned out to be most exciting. We got the lumber for it off the beach. We located the tub as near the edge of the point as we possibly could and surrounded it with windows. It was not enough for us seafarin' ones, however, to commune with the gulls as they flew past, we had to see them overhead too, so daddy arranged for a sliding skylight. In summer we pushed it back and lay in the hot soapy water, looking straight up into the deep blue. White pelicans and gulls sailing along added an element of chance. In the winter the view was the same, only safer.

The floor, we made from flat blue flagstones laboriously dragged from the beach below. Daddy undertook the plumbing. He got to the point of joining a pipe onto another one out over the 250-foot cliff.

Carefully, he tied a rope around his waist and knotted it securely. Then he tied it around a fig tree in the patio. Over the side he bounded with all of us standing audiencing. He was lithe and agile as he leapt from one small rock to another and won a footing. Mama looked away when daddy got extra jumpy. The job was almost done when Bungy walked over to the edge of the point and shouted, "Daddy, kin' I have this wope' to tie up my horse wif'?"

"Sure," agreed daddy magnanimously – then "Wait a minute! Isn't hat the rope that's around my waist?"

"Yes," answered Bungy, "but I'll use the wope' that's around the tree."

"Hell's bells!" screamed daddy. "Aren't they the same?"

"No," confessed Bungy, "I'm holding the end of yours."

Mama's face blanched when she realized what daddy had done. He had tied one rope around his waist – another to the tree.

Work was over for that day – as daddy clung desperately to a protruding root while we made his rope secure. As soon as he could, he scrambled up, puffing and blowing.

His only words were, "Ignorance is indeed bliss, isn't it?"

CHAPTER 11

That summer Bungy and I began to collect cats. Unfeeling persons brought sacks of them out of town and dumped them over our cliff. Of course, we couldn't bear to hear their pitiful mewing without doing something. The something was to bring them up and give them some milk – they were so cute.

Beowulf and Beethoven were the favorites. Beowulf had a litter of four kittens one day. How happy and proud she was! Her black, shiny fur got blacker and shinier. Daddy was stern and unrelenting about us not bringing up any more cats. There were thousands running around the place already.

One day at dusk Bungy and I heard the familiar frantic meowing. We dashed down the cliff, rescued the dear little things from the tied sack, and carried them in our arms to the house. When we reached the gate we stopped terrified that daddy might see them. Miserably, we looked around for a place to hide them – Beowulf nursing her own little brood! The very thing – we placed them gently by her side, she nudged them smellingly; they caught on to a tit somewhere, and the whole group was a picture of contentment.

Later that night daddy came in scratching his head. "I thought Beowulf had only four kittens," he said. "She's sure got eight of them now." We children didn't look up from our drawing.

That Hallowe'en, Arthur and Beulah Kearns brought us a hug box of costumes. Arthur worked for a movie rental house and ever so often they went through their clothing, sorting some of it out to be burned. Arthur and Beulah didn't have any children, but they certainly had mama and papa souls. They always knew what would make us the happiest.

In California "trick or treat" is the rage on Hallowe'en. You dress up in a costume, go to a door, knock on it and when the man of the house answers, you say "Trick or treat?" He surprises you by bringing out an apple or orange or candy or nuts. To pay him you don't soap his windows, or tear up his gate or anything.

We called our playroom out at one end of the garden the map room because we'd papered it with maps. We took the costumes out there, emerging shortly as Mary, Queen of Scots, a fairy, a pirate, and an Eskimo. The Ba was that and Mary, Queen of Scots, carried her on her back, in a papoose board. Off we went "trick or treating."

Mama stayed home to mend, daddy to read. Ever so often throughout the evening, an arm flashed through the door leaving fruit or some kind of goody until the pile was tremendous.

The last time a hand shot in, mama caught a glimpse of an angel flitting past the portholes.

"I didn't know any of our children were angels," said mama.

"They're not; they're usually devils," daddy mumbled, looking up from his book. "Er' what's that you say?"

"An angel just flew past the port hole; it looked like Flo Ann. When I saw her she was Mary, Queen of Scots."

"Definitely not an angel," opinioned daddy. "Something is wrong."

They made their way to the map room and threw back the door. Costumes from far-flung countries were flung far and near. It was evident to our parents that we had been working hard at this "trick or treat" business, changing characters often and making the rounds over and over. That accounted for the tremendous pile. When we came in, daddy lectured us on honesty while mama sat and looked solemn. When we went to bed, we heard them laughing and laughing and wondered what on earth about.

In a family the size of ours somebody's birthday is always coming along. Bungy's did. Mama spent quite a while in the kitchen, the morning of the twenty-first of November, fixing the lunch. She opened a good many cupboard doors and tin boxes, but closed them again quickly. Finally she came out with a not too big basket and a not too big box. "Here is our picnic lunch," she said, handing the basket to daddy, and "here," to Flo Ann, "is Bungy's birthday cake." We all wanted to carry it, but whoever did had to be careful as we walked over the slippery, mossy rocks, on our way to Point Fermin. The sun played hide and seek among fluffs of fog which looked like pink cotton candy. Sometimes we could tell the sea was near only by its voice and by the little white waves that ran up and lapped our ankles.

When we reached the sheltered place under the cliff, where the old lighthouse is, we built a fire, so the potatoes could be put on to boil. Mama got out six red tomatoes that daddy had found in a farmer's deserted field and arranged them to mark our places around a big flat rock. She took the cake out of the box and put it in the center. It was little but beautiful. It had Happy Birthday written in red hots on the top.

All day long we children played in the tide pools, while daddy brought in debris off the beach. Mama said we should think about how thrilling it was that we were picnicking on soil five hundred million years old. "You have trod where the dinosaur has trod," said mama in a stagey voice as she showed us the prehistoric tracks on the rocks.

Bungy played some with her rope doll that daddy had made her. It had shell eyes.

When golden streaks began to play on the water and gulls began to get extra ambitious and squawky over a disputed fish dinner, daddy said, "We'd better eat now; we've got a long walk ahead of us."

Everything tasted good.   The peanut butter and cracker sandwiches were still crispy.

After we'd eaten every morsel of cake, Bungy said, "When we're rich, at somebody's birthday, let's go to Long Beach and ride on the merry-go-round."   Mama looked at the sky, the moon cradling a little star in the west, the earth and all of us. "We're rich now, little Bungy," she said as she drew us into her arms.   "Oh, yes, oh, yes, we're rich, we're rich," we shouted exuberantly as we rose and began to dance around Bungy, singing "Happy Birthday to you, Happy birthday to you, Happy Birthday, dear Bungy, Happy Birthday to you."

When we reached Little House, mama got out the picture album we'd brought from Oklahoma. "Here's one of Marilyn on a Shetland pony.   Here's Flo when she was a baby in Carrie's arms on Danelson Lake.   That's Cody rowing the boat.   Here's one of a birthday party in our garden.   There's James Warner Smith, Edward Grisso, Lynn, Alan and Beverly Chase, Mary Joy and Wallace Craig, the Lancaster girls, Rusty Norvel, and our children, Eli," she said.

"What's that thing?" asked Bungy.

"That's the cake!" answered mama.

"What a big birthday cake!" Bungy's voice was awed.

Mama closed the book quietly and walked away.

CHAPTER 12

It was about this time that mama lost her conventions and life became more simple. One night there was phosphorous on the water. The moon was a big red orange, as it crept languorously over the point. In Oklahoma we would have called it a harvest moon. Here its only harvest was beauty as it darted and slid in and out of the waves, making the algae streaks of lightning on the water.

Our Japanese neighbors, the Kawashiris, had brought us dozens of ears of sweet corn. We boiled them in big pot on the beach and ate until we couldn't eat any more. We lay for a while in the soft darkness. A buoy signed mournfully. A gull screamed raucously. Little crabs made a crunching noise as they edged backwards over the rocks. Phosphorous flashed and shone like silver.

Daddy broke the spell. "Who's ready for a swim?" he said, rising quickly and pulling mama up by the hand. Flo and Bungy followed. Soon they were squealing and laughing. I stayed on the sand with The Ba and wrote a poem. It was:

I love the sea

Not as a swimmer loves the sea,

Bracing himself for the icy plunge,

Feeling the sun warm gently his back

Slapping the water into water spouts –

Gaily cavorting in seaweed sarong.

I love the sea,

Much as a friend loves a friend,

Trying to understand her moods,

Failing to do so, loving her still,

Loving her mighty rage in a storm,

Her gentle motherliness at sunset,

The little sea things asleep at her breast.

It wasn't good but it made me feel good. The swimmers were quieter as they settled down to steady swimming. They looked like a beautiful ballet as their shiny bodies rolled rhythmically.

Then it was, mama said, that she lost her conventions. Before this "They" had held and bound her. She hadn't wanted to feel that way but her bringing up had made her accept the general opinion of "They" as conclusive and not to be questioned. Consequently, certain people and races were to be considered possibilities as friends, others were not.

As she swam that night, something began to happen to her. Suddenly her heart nearly broke as she thought of the times she had let Carrie trudge home in the snow, wearing only threadbare clothes, a brown cotton stocking on her head, and shoes with holes in the soles.

How could she have not asked Mrs. Kawashiri in to rest as she stood at the door with the corn? What difference did it make if mama herself had to wash Ba's diapers and hang them out to dry without Carrie's help? Suddenly she saw the inside of everybody instead of the outside. She laughed right out loud as she thought of the fun she was going to have now since "They" didn't matter any more; it was like waking from a troubled sleep.

When the dripping ones were drying themselves around a big bonfire, daddy said glowingly, "Malcolm, what's happened? You look so pretty."

Mama said, "Do I? I feel like Scrooge when we awoke and found it was Christmas day. Tomorrow we're going to call on the Kawashiris."

The next morning we caught mama peering ecstatically through a space between boards behind the cook stove. "Just think," she said, "some people don't have a kitchen with cracks large enough to see a sailing ship go by."

Then we got it settled about time. Daddy had sold his and mama's wrist watches to get money for food. Our cuckoo clock had got bounced around so much it wouldn't run right. It still cuckooed and that's all we cared about. When our friends came down from Hollywood, they always wanted to know – after the "hello's" and "how are you's" – "What time is it?" It embarrassed us when we couldn't tell them. "Oh, never mind, I didn't really want to know anyway," they'd say. We began to philosophize on whether they really did want to know or whether it made them feel better to ask. We decided to make an experiment.

The day came when another friend wanted the time. Daddy gave it to him, the first "time" that popped into his head. "Thanks," mumbled our friend – and went right on talking. Intermittently throughout the day daddy gave him false "times." We children could hold our giggles no longer when toward evening daddy countered with, "What time is it, Joe?"

Joe took out his watch, looked at it carefully and replied, "Thirteen o'clock, Eli." He had, at last, caught on.

Afterwards, daddy delivered his lecture. "Now, girls," he said, "time can be convenient. Often it's a bore. Never, never let it boss you."

You might think from what I've written so far that our days were filled with aimless enjoyment. Far from it! When Harry and Ruth Tobey came down from Studio City for a rest and went with us in the morning beachcombing, fished with us in the afternoon off the rocks, carried in wood for the fireplace that night, and finally fell into bed exhausted, Harry dryly remarked, "You lead the busiest life doing nothing I've ever seen."

Little House was a beehive of activity. All of us lived with hammers and nails and paintbrushes. All kinds of changes were going on. We decided from the first that we'd copy no one. Originality was the necessity. We grew more and more infatuated with the beauty we found on the beach. Here was an art, strange and mysterious. No human hand could have given such character to a sea-swept cork, nor could have etched so delicately a piece of driftwood.

Best of all we liked beachcombing in the rain. We liked the friendly feeling of raindrops as they pattered gently our upturned faces or pelted urgently our bowed heads and shoulders. We liked the black seaweed waving in the tide pools. We felt close to the little crabs as they scurried about looking for another wave to carry them home. We liked to look at the sea gulls as they soared and screamed above our heads. A flash of white breast, an orange-colored bill, and a wing's curve is a beautiful thing on a rainy morning. They flew so gracefully above the snowy crest of a gray wave, that the sight made us stop dead in our tracks and marvel at such loveliness. One rainy morning, the beach below Point Fermin was strewn with barrels, big, medium-sized, and little. All day we worked, carrying them to Little House a mile away. Soon daddy began to make barrel things, and Flo and I furnished a room with them.

CHAPTER 13

Then mama and daddy had a long talk. Should daddy get himself a job so that his family might have security? Was food more important than fun? What would we children grow up to be if life kept being such a precarious, hazardous, delightful adventure? They both agreed that there was only one sensible thing to do – daddy must get a job the next day.

In the morning, Hideko, Setsuko, Udeko, and Chio Kawashiri knocked on the door. They were on their way for abalones. If we'd come along, they'd show us how to pry them off the rock. Daddy couldn't wait to get his pants on.

Mr. Fred Back of Farmer's Market fame in his book, Second Carrot from the End, mentions abalone cooking. Now I will tell of abalone getting. Contrary to opinion, you don't always have to dive for them – although you usually get wet. They lie on the side of a rock, pressing themselves gently to its surface. Any iron flat piece, sharp on one end, will do for prying. You sort of catch them unawares in tide pools when the tide is out and one jab of your crowbar will dislodge them if you use it before they have a chance to clamp themselves on tightly, which they do at the slightest provocation. You can keep them for a day in wet seaweed, but it's better to relieve them of their beautiful shells immediately. They quiet down after that. Cut off the outside edge, slice them cross wise and start pounding with a hammer or any old thing. See that the muscle is broken down completely before you dip them in beaten eggs and cracker crumbs – and put them in a skillet containing hot, hot fat.

I never have timed the cooking. Mr. Beck said eight seconds – he's probably right – Just long enough to brown on one side, whist! over and brown on the other side. I know that long cooking makes them tough because I tried that one time. That night, we ate abalones. The words "steady" and "job" were taboo around our house after that.

On a cold rainy day in December mama sold her rings. The place where they had been was white and funny. We were all sad but daddy was the saddest. He stared and stared at her fingers.

"Never mind, dearest," said mama. "Tomorrow we'll go to Olvera Street and get a Mexican silver wedding ring, and this time it will be more thrilling than it was before because this time I'll know how lucky I am to get you. Before, I only guessed."

The next day when they came home from the City of the Angels mama proudly showed us her ring and told us all about their trip to the oldest part of the city. She said, if you stopped at the entrance of the little Olvera Street and closed your eyes and tried hard, you could sort of recapture the spirit of old Los Angeles, whatever that was.

The chestnuts roasting on charcoal smelled so good, the dirty cats rubbing around your ankles were so friendly, Jose Herrera making candles at number 27½ was so interesting, patiently pouring his steaming wax over and over strings hanging from an iron hoop. The little Mexican children, looking like Leo Politi paintings, amused her the most with their broken Spanish interspersed with "O.K., Kid."

She and daddy found a wonderful place to eat. A little hole in the wall with doors made of rough branches laced together with leather straps. In the center of the room was an old tree growing out of the cobblestone floor. In one corner was a small shrine, on top of it were paper flowers – a candle burned low in a broken glass, lighting up a sweet-faced Mary done by some peasant artist. The owner and cook, one and the same, a beautiful Mexican woman, dished out enchiladas, tacos, and fried beans with a haughty expression.

After dinner they found a little shop and bought candied apples and pecan pralines for us children. When we ate them, they tasted so good and sugary, and we were happy that mama's finger looked natural again.

CHAPTER 14

If an impressionistic painter had been trying to put us on paper at this time, he would probably have had a series of jagged mountains and dark, sad valleys. There seemed to have been no level places at all. At times, we were intoxicated with the richness of this life we were living by the sea and at others cast into the depths by the poverty of it. We couldn't have made it without friends.

There was Uncle Wyatt, tall and handsome, dry and humorous. There was Aunty Louise confined to a wheel chair but as fresh and piquant as a mint julep.

There was Uncle Ralph who sang us to sleep in a sweet nasal voice with naughty French songs which he had learned during the First World War. There was Aunty Ethel who sparkled and bubbled enthusiastically. She hated the martyrs. The only way we could repay her for all the things she did for us was to pretend that she never did anything. Aunty Ethel thought any situation could be made better by a cozy session with a piece of cinnamon toast and tea – and I ask you, can't it?

There was little rotund Dick Elliot, movie actor and pepper-upper extraordinary, who brought us popcorn and candy. We thought he stole every scene in the movies he was in even if he only walked through. There was Esther, his wife, who brought mama a white satin evening gown, which she'd made from odds and ends, she said. Mama dressed for dinner several times and sat around darning socks afterwards, looking satiny and shimmery. Her eyes shown, too. Esther had a very understanding heart.

There was Grace Walker, a rebel against all the laws of "you have to do it this way because this is the way it's always been done before." She was a school teacher, but managed to act less like it than Puck himself. When Grace visited us, it was like living a fairy story. Humdrum things ceased to exist.

There was Marion Stockton, who flew into everything even if it was scrambling eggs as though her life depended on it. (By the way, she added a little Worcester sauce to her supper eggs, and yummy!) She made the most beautiful flower arrangements. Sometimes she used weeds and vegetables. They made the pretties bouquets of all. She and her husband, Cecil, who was handsome in a homely way and reminded us of Abraham Lincoln, built a house out of an old garage in the wrong part of town. They made it so adorable that half of Los Angeles had beaten a path to its doors to visit with its owners and view Marion's exquisite pottery. One time when our pipes had burst and we were without water, Marion and Cecil brought us some. They stood at the front door singing, to the tune of "How Dry I Am":

Somebody knows
How dry you are,
So here we come
Down with our jar.

We'd give our coat,
Our hat, our shoes,
For friends like youse

And youse and youse.

There was Elizabeth Sale, authoress, and poetry editor of Rob Wagner's Beverly Hills *Script,* who defied everything, especially description. A heart as big as all outdoors and a laugh the same. She ran Henry VIII a close second for robust humor. Perhaps she described herself best when she said she was an atheist with a Christian viewpoint. She joined a church after much trembling of spirit because she thought the pastor was an intelligent man and she wanted to help him with his membership drive. The first Sunday after she became a member, she arose bright and early hell bent (her own words) for services. As she went down the steps, she fell and sprained her ankle. "See," she said bitterly, "that's what I get for joining the church."

She told us about her little grandson who came to live with her. "He'd been taught by his mother's family that he was an angel and the stork changed him into a baby and dropped him down the chimney. Odds Zodds, what drivel. I grabbed up Van Loon's *History of Mankind,* showed him a monkey, telling him that's what he used to look like. He was delighted!" Elizabeth shrieked with laughter. "He loves monkeys!"

There was Betsey, Bungy's best friend, who was the way she was, I guess, because she had Hans and Tula for a papa and mama. Of all the people we knew, they understood best how to live. A meal in their house was never just another meal. It was an event. Among the pieces of Norwegian furniture hundreds of years old, the Gudes' graciousness was hospitality at its best. There were the Hardwicks, who mama said were as nutty as we were, only nicer. The house they lived in was much nicer. A formal, dignified Colonial type, located at Doheny Canyon. Mrs. Hardwick was a lovely blonde and a born party giver. Any gathering of more than two people, at her direction, became a gay "affair." Mr. Hardwick liked to carve at the table but hated candles.

One Thanksgiving day we were invited to their house for dinner. It was served at five o'clock in the afternoon so we children could be among those present. The draperies were drawn, tall yellow candles in silver candle-stocks gave a soft, a very soft light. Mr. Hardwick groaned, "We'll need cat's eyes to find our places in this light, or rather dark."

Mrs. Hardwick smiled sweetly, ignoring that remark. Amid laughter and conversation, we seated ourselves. Vashti, their colored cook, sprang in with the turkey, placing it in front of Mr. Hardwick. He reached in his pocket, took out his specs, put them on his nose, and said, "Oh, here it is!" Mrs. Hardwick talked on, again ignoring him. He picked up his fork, jabbed it into its breast. Juice spouted and to everyone's horror, the turkey left the platter and sailed through the air, plop onto the floor. Vashti rose to the occasion. With a wild shout, she grabbed it up in her arms and flew to the kitchen. Before you could say Jack Robinson, she had reappeared, carrying a clean plate, on which the turkey rested. She glided over to the table, slid the turkey into its garnish nest, and said with great dignity, "I found this in the other room, suh. I thought maybe you could use it."

Easter made mama think of the Hardwicks. When we were living in our dark tourist court, Mrs. Hardwick gave a party. Everything was white and shiny, the flowers fragrant and dewy. Mama said she felt like she had risen from the tomb or had been born again or something awfully Eastery.

CHAPTER 15

By this time our patio and outdoor workshop was filled to overflowing with what can be picked up on the beach. Rusty anchors, crusted with pink barnacles, life preservers gray with the buffeting of the sea and wind, reams of dark brown fishnet, all weaves, tuna, sardine, anchovy, and barracuda. Net needles, slick from lying buried in the sand, fish floats of blue, amber, and amethyst glass, driftwood, beautiful, bizarre, and grotesque, star fishes (little fishes shaped like stars, aren't they wonderful really!) and silvery corks strung on chocolate brown rope.

Daddy had made fisherman's candle lamps, hurricane lanterns, and old Sea Scout goblets. He had taken the top ends of saki bottles and stuck them into corks for these.

One night the wind howled around Little House and sneaked in under the doors and around the windows. The rain lashed and whipped the roof. Dinner was only potato soup. We didn't even have biscuits. After dinner, daddy sat with his head in his hands for a long time. Suddenly he asked, "This is all so beautiful. These things from the sea, I mean. Do you think anyone would buy them?"

"I believe someone would," mama answered earnestly. "Beauty is as important as potatoes."

"But it's really junk," countered daddy. Mama was not to be downed. "Beautiful junk embellished with ideas," she said.

"Would you be afraid to go with me tomorrow to see if I can sell it?"

"Whither thou goest, goest I," misquoted mama; and so, a business was born!

The next morning the little truck was loaded again, this time with sea colorfulness. Away went mama and daddy to see if there was a place where people would pay for beauty. Daddy could not resist stopping at a shabby, nautically trimmed nightclub. A dirty, fat man with a tooth pick in his mouth came out, looked at the load, then at mama and daddy, scratched his head and asked, "What you aimin' to do with this junk?"

"I was aimin' on selling it," answered daddy.

The man laughed and laughed. Mama's cheeks burned and daddy drove off as fast as he could in the Model A.

"Well, that settled one thing," said mama. "That isn't the place."

As they drove into the city, daddy mused. "In one way, the load does look like junk. What is it that makes it so fascinating? Imagination! That's it! You have to see something of what is in your heart in the stuff. One thing is sure. We must take it where there is imagination."

"Let's try Bullock's Wilshire," said mama.

The little truck stopped across the street from the big store. "I can't make myself take this car into the parking lot where the footman is," said daddy. He got out of the car, slammed the door with a tinny bang, pulled down his coat, straightened his tie, took mama's hand in his, leaned over to kiss it, and said, "Till we meet again, my sweet."

Mama was too scared to say anything. There were butterflies, humming birds, and maybe a few woodpeckers in her stomach.

During daddy's absence, she sat drawn into a knot, stiffly waiting for – whatever was going to happen.

Soon she saw daddy and two men coming across the street, chatting pleasantly. Daddy introduced them as Mr. Parker and Mr. Dexter, in charge of displays. They were charming, both of them, and loved the load of "beauty." Bought all of it for $40.00 and ordered more. Mama and daddy were walking on air when they returned, with the story of their trip, great plans in their heads, and $39.00 in their pockets. They'd stopped to celebrate on their way home. Hamburgers, everything on them!

CHAPTER 16

When we awoke the next morning, we had the "Christmas feeling." And why not, with $39.00 in the house? We must have looked threadbare and shabby as we followed the path that runs along the top of the Cliff to Point Firmin light house, but we had never felt so rich and happy. There was something about daddy getting money for the beauty we had so much fun collecting, that made us exuberant. It all seemed so right to be rewarded for having fun. We were on our way to catch the bus which went into San Pedro. We were going to get New Shoes! Flo, Bungy, and I wanted sturdy brown oxfords. They weren't hard to find, but we hunted quite a while for The Ba's. After all, mama said, an elf must have elf shoes. We finally found them, tiny, black patent leather Roman sandals. Daddy met us at noon for "Coney Islands." He took us to the wharf where the fishing fleet was docked. Fishermen were mending tan barked nets. Sometimes they cut out large pieces because the net was too worn to hold a big fish. They threw away corks that could no longer be depended on to float. Old corks and net were what we wanted now since we were in the beachcombing business. Daddy made a deal with them. Everything they threw off the mending dock was his.

In a few days, daddy had collected enough beauty to make a second trip into town. He decided to take twice as much as Bullock's Wilshire had ordered. He'd sell it to some other store. Then he struck on a few more pieces, just in case. Mr. Parker and Mr. Dexter met him with open arms. They were going to do the whole store in beachcomber motif come summer. They'd want some more things.

When daddy left them, he stayed on Wilshire until he came to Desmond's in the Miracle Mile. "This is a nice store," he thought. He drove up into the alley to the delivery door, getting bolder now. It didn't take the buyer over ten minutes to decide he had to have this sea glory, but if daddy wanted his money, he'd have to go to the downtown store on Broadway to get it. It was four o'clock. No checks were issued after four-thirty. To the heart of Los Angeles, dashed daddy in the rattletrap truck. He made it, just in time. Such success made daddy jubilant. This was fun! He dug out the extra things, arranging them provocatively on top of some fish net in the truck. He drove west toward Beverly Hills. On La Cienga Avenue, he parked in front of the "Tail of the Cock" Café and went to the hamburger hut across the street for a cup of coffee. When he came out, he saw two men standing by the car. "Now, I've done it," sighed daddy. "I never should have stopped that tin can there." With a sinking heart, he made his way through the traffic and came up apologetically. One of the men introduced himself as manager of the restaurant. The other was a Mr. Vaughn.

"These are attractive things," said the latter. "Are they for sale?"

"Yes," gulped daddy.

"I'm making a playroom in my house and decorating it as a French wine cellar. I'd like to buy these lamps and goblets if you don't mind doing a curbstone business. Could you help me carry them in to show to my wife?

Daddy followed him, his arms loaded helter skelter. A very beautiful lady admired them with a sweet soprano voice. She wanted a few changes here and there. Daddy went outside, sat down, changed ropes, nails, and net. People looked wonderingly at the man sitting on the curb in front of the "Tail of the Cock" café working with a net needle on fish net, but daddy didn't care. He had learned that the sweet-voiced one was none other than Deanna Durbin!

Daddy was delirious when he reached Little House with a gardenia for mama, hair ribbons for us girls, and a chocolate éclair all around. What a business! What customers! What excitement! We had so much money, we didn't know what to do with it! And orders!

About this time we had the storm! Daddy says there are two kinds of people in the world, those who can live without seasons and those who cannot. Seasons give nature a personality. Winter is a living thing. It talks with you, battles with you, and throws snow balls at you. Spring is soft and alluring. It puts all kinds of ideas into your head and heart. Its singing winds lift you right up to the sky. Summer is a queen, regal, shining, motherly. Summer is an open book revealing nature's secrets. Autumn is a memory, chuck full of everything worth remembering, both the sad and the gay. Autumn looks backward while it goes forward.

A storm in California makes up to us for not having seasons. The one that broke upon us that winter made up for everything. For days, we heard an ominous roar. Our mother sea was warning us. Finally the tempest was upon us. The world was purple, the water green, trimmed with sizzling white foam. One wall of wave after another crashed and spent itself on the rocks. We lived in a dream world. Little House rocked back and forth, the window panes rattled and shook.

We were as spent and tired as the sea when the blow was over. One morning, mauve skies were shaded with pink. The sun coming up over the harbor cast long, worshipping arms heavenward. A formation of white-breasted sandpipers looked like a huge butterfly flitting and dipping in the air. The beach was a treasure chest. We worked all day gathering loveliness from among the wet debris cast up by the raging waters. A good storm is a boon to a beachcomber.

After a storm we go beachcombing for boats. Daddy makes furniture out of our finds more than he travels in them. The usually sleek yachts and neat little boats that ride in the harbor at anchor look disheveled and unneat the day after a blow. Some of them can never be used again and these are the ones daddy grabs. Once we found one too big for loading on our trailer. Flo Ann insisted that we row it home, a distance of two sea miles, around Point Firmin, to White Point and into our little harbor. Flo Ann is the most convincing person you ever saw, when she wants to be. Her arguments sound so sound while she's talking. I gave in and decided to go along. Before we were well out of the harbor we knew we'd made a mistake. We had caulked the holes, but new ones sprang up all over the bottom. The bailing became more strenuous than the rowing. It seemed to us that whoever was at the oars never moved the boat an inch. We couldn't decide what was best to do. To abandon ship and swim back would be a hard, a maybe too hard grind. I'm not a deep sea swimmer like Flo Ann. If we kept rowing, the boat might go under anyway and we'd be in a worse predicament because we'd be farther out in open sea.

Bailing had become a frantic back and forth process to keep the water below sinking line. Never let it be said that Flo Ann is not an old salt. She sized up the situation, stroked her chin exactly as though it were covered with whiskers, and said coolly, "I'll tell you, matey, an old sea dog always sticks to the boat. Let's follow his example." I knew she was funny but I couldn't laugh. We were making a little headway, as we cleared the harbor and attempted to swing over as close to the rocky shore as possible, in the hope that we might find some place to land our rickety craft. As we rounded Point Firmin, my heart gave a great leap because in the distance I saw two men fishing from the rocks. I could have sworn they had on shining armour which knights wear! "Help!" I screamed. "Help!" Flo Ann shouted "Ahoy!" They must have discerned our plight because they immediately plunged in through the breakers and started toward us.

Within fifteen minutes we and the boat were safely ashore. As the swimmers dragged our craft onto the rocks, Flo was still madly rowing, I was still madly bailing. That's the last time we ever rowed one of daddy's wrecks home.

That boat was an eight-footer. He made a couch out of it, using real springs so it could be used for an extra bed, and upholstered it with handwoven fish net material.

Daddy used another boat as a cupboard to hold books and knick-knacks. It stood against the wall, a ship's lantern hanging in its bow, its shelves loaded with books. In fact, I can't think of anything daddy hasn't made from a broken-down, thrown-away boat.

CHAPTER 17

All this time daddy made regular trips into town. He beat a path to the door of every department store; in fact, wherever he felt there was imagination. It was a funny thing about that. Daddy could tell by looking at anyone whether he was going to like his creations (daddy hates that word) or not. He could tell when a prospective buyer was going to be a customer because he always laughed when he saw the lamps, goblets, old chests, and so forth. It was because they were so evidently made from nothing. This fact always seemed amusing. Daddy insisted that all he had to sell was an idea. The buyer supplied the rest out of his own experiences. Daddy got very philosophic after he started selling. I think he was really trying to explain people buying his works to himself, but to tell you the truth, he is still scratching his head.

One day we found Russ. Russ was the exact opposite of daddy. Russ had tools, daddy, had none; Russ knew what time it was, daddy never did; Russ knew how to cut a straight line, daddy didn't; Russ kept track of his hammer, daddy lost his. Russ kept his feet on the ground, daddy had his head and feet both in the clouds. Daddy told Russ his dream. Russ said, "It cain't be done." Then, "Ah, now, I say it cain't, maybe it kin'. Let me see." After a session with a ruler and square, he thought it could. Russ was a big help, still is. Without Russ the horse they figured out would probably not have held together at all. The horse was the cutest thing, made of driftwood, with palm front legs, frayed rope mane and tail. He had white clam-shell eyelids with fish-net eyelashes. Window trimmers especially loved him. He began to show up all over Los Angeles with beads around his neck, a hat on his head, being petted by models, and all sorts of ways.

Daddy and Ray Hunter then got together. He put out a bulletin on Eli, depicting him as an old gray-bearded, salty beachcomber. We fixed the little horse as a bar, for his trade, placing a tray on his back to hold goblets, and side packs for bottles of ginger ale.

For some time daddy had been thinking about the movies. Why wouldn't this colorful flotsam be an answer to the set dresser's need for atmosphere? Away Eli went, without the faintest idea of how he was going to get inside the studios. He had heard that he could not possibly crash the gates without an introduction of some kind. Columbia's set department opens onto the street. He figured he'd have the best chance there. Daddy whisked up to the door in the tin can and gave his name to an affable, gray-haired doorman. "Hedley," mused the old gentleman. "I knew a Hedley in Holdenville, Oklahoma."

"My brother Tom," shouted Daddy.

"My brother's daughter married George Eckels of that city." Doorman Mr. Howell beamed.

"I know him," daddy said. "He was a member of the Cockle Burr bachelors club, too."

"It's a small world, isn't it?" said the nice old man as he put his arm around daddy's shoulders and ushered him into the sacred confines of Columbia's inner sanctum. The set dresser bought his entire load. Some of it was used later for scenes in the moving picture, "Cover Girl." We were listening to a radio broadcast one night and heard an academy award being given to the art director for his café scenes in that picture. The café was full of our beach. We sort of basked in reflected glory.

But Daddy couldn't find a friend of a friend everywhere. Metro-Goldwyn-Mayer's gates were closed so tightly that he couldn't find a crack. He talked to the "set man" over the telephone from the office. It was impossible to describe "pure poetry of line." Words were too dull. The man didn't get it. Daddy was denied admittance. He went back to the little truck, brooding and plotting. Daddy was getting bolder. Soon he saw the policeman, with whom he had talked, leave and a fresh one take his place. Daddy rattled up to the front gate and sang out of the corner of his mouth, "Fish net for the property department."

The officer looked at the load and bawled back, "Straight ahead, to your right, to your left, right again, and straight ahead for four blocks."

"Thanks," said daddy, but he was thinking, "Gosh, this is a big place." Finally arriving, daddy took two old ship's lamps, and strode through the door. He was met by Jack Hines, who looked at him suspiciously. "What you got there?" he asked.

"Ship's lamps," answered Daddy. "They're for sale."

"Oh, yeah," Jack parried. "Maybe you got some skeletons, too – huh?

Daddy had heard stories about how crazy there were in the movies and he was about to believe them all, when Jack bellowed, "Where did you get those lamps?"

Daddy is not big, but he was born in Texas and that makes up for a lot of things. "That," he said, "is none of your business."

"Tell me one thing," Jack said. "Did you get them from our property department?"

"I did not," said daddy and told him the truth. Jack then explained his actions.

A few weeks before a man had come with a skeleton for sale. The property department was overjoyed as that item is scarce. Jack's exultation knew no bounds, when the second time that week a skeleton was offered for sale. Two skeletons in one week was really progress. Mrs. Hines went around bragging about it all over the lot. You can imagine his chagrin when he read in the little studio paper, "Jack Hines buys his own skeleton." Some office wags had known his glee at buying the first one and had sold the same one to him again. Daddy's lamps were exactly like some Jack had already in his possession. That, coupled with the fact that no one had announced daddy, made his suspicions flare. After that he and daddy got on famously and we supplied Metro-Goldwyn-Mayer with our beachcombings right along.

Every studio in Hollywood needed some part of our beach at one time or another. Paramount turned our way when Dorothy Lamour made a picture. "Rainbow Island" was a hey-day for us. One day, Warner Brothers' big truck appeared at the front gate of Little House. We didn't have a telephone. The art director was in a hurry, so he had sent the driver with a list. We loaded him down with everything we could find and half stripped the dining room. After he left, daddy rushed around with paper and pencil, acting for all the world like "Big Business."

Our days became purposeful indeed. After school, time was given wholly to helping daddy on the beach. Heavenly pickings were ours.

Daddy decided to try the photographers, and that's how we got our pictures in the American Magazine. In making the rounds he came to Mr. Dick Whittington who didn't want any fish net but thought daddy's business was interesting. He came down to Little House and took a picture of us all, lined up on the mast of the derelict S.S. Herriman, which had washed in after the ship was scuttled at sea a few miles out. Mr. Whittington and his son Ed were nice and we had a good time at tea. He was sorry we didn't get several pages, but mama confided to us that she was glad there was only one picture. "Publicity is a cheap, common thing." (But now, I think she actually looks forward to seeing her family's name and pictures in print because I know she went to see herself in the same movie short three times.)

Mr. Whitington and his son Ed were nice. We had a good tea. He came down to Little House and took a picture of us all lined up on the mast of derelict "S.S. Heriman" for an article which appeared in "American Magazine."

CHAPTER 18

It would have been nice if in this account I could have given you exact dates for happenings. I mentioned this to mama when I started writing. For days she juggled figures and chewed off the ends of several pencils. Marriage 19??, First child 19??, Fire 19??, Came to California 19??. "Now I'll put this paper where I won't lose it," she declared victoriously.

When I was ready for it, mama had forgotten where she had hidden it. We hunted but were never able to find it. If you could have seen the look on her face when I suggested another list, you wouldn't blame me for not. New Year's rolled in every January 1, however, until came the date, hard for even mama to forget, December 7, 1941.

The European rumble had been loud enough to be heard in Little House for some time. Isolated as we were, we yet felt very close to it all, and none of us had ever considered it "not our business." A feeling of uneasiness and sadness ran through our joy over daddy's selling his beauty.

On that Sunday which seems so long ago mama and daddy went to a musical tea in San Pedro, and mama had a new hat. When the news of the attack on Pearl Harbor was announced over the radio, we children didn't believe it. We thought it was more Orson Welles realism. The news came again and again. Finally we understood! It was true! Our neighbors, the Kawashiris! They were Japanese! How dreadful they must feel! We ran out of the house and met Kioshi coming our way. He was ten years old with rosy red cheeks. His eyes hardly slanted a bit. He was the son of a high school football hero. A few days before we had laughed at him for being so "American." He showed daddy how the Japanese people wrote. "See," he said, "they write up and down on the paper, like this; while we write across the paper, like this." As far as he was concerned, "we" meant Americans.

Now his eyes were nearly popping out of his head. "Have you heard?" he stuttered. "They bombed Honolulu." Behind him came Setsuke, age thirteen. She was crying quietly. "Don't cry, don't cry, Setsuke!" we moaned.

None of the rest of the Kawashiris showed themselves that day. Mama and daddy came home at five o'clock. They had to go way around to get to White Point, as the Army had taken over Paseo del Mar, the walk along the sea. How quickly they had closed it off, with barbed wire and armed guards. The war seemed very real. An atmosphere of tenseness pervaded the harbor district, especially the west end of Paseo del Mar.

There were Japanese families all around us. One day the report came that the army had bought a huge portion of land including that on which was beloved Little House. Heavens, we'd have to move!

One night Los Angeles was attacked – remember? We were awakened by big guns booming and the wailing of sirens. Running to the window, we saw the most beautiful sight. The heavens were ablaze with things going off, exactly like a large scale Fourth of July without restrictions. Such fun couldn't be dangerous. We ran out into the patio shouting. Daddy strode through the gate, threw out his arms and stated heroically – "It has come, at last. This is war."

The next morning the papers were a little vague about what had come. The reports became vaguer, even though the Secretary of War announced that enemy planes had been sighted. We finally concluded that the jitters had caused the Army to stage a gigantic, colossal, tremendous show, with the whole city as a credulous spectator.

Came the day our Japanese neighbors and friends joined their countrymen to form the caravan which rolled slowly along to Santa Anita and other relocation centers. We, with their other San Pedro friends, saw them off. Mr. Seo, an awfully old man, kept pumping our hands up and down, saying "We come back, when it's finish'." Hideko made a joke about which horse's stall she'd occupy at Santa Anita. Setsuko sat still, her head bowed down, and stroked her dog Tana's ears. She had given him to the soldiers stationed on White Point for the duration.

We felt so lonely when they had gone, restless and unsettled too, as we knew we'd have to go somewhere soon. Mama started her little game with the representative of the Attorney General. The first time he called, he tried to warn us of what would come. The Army would eventually "take over." Mama smiled sweetly, told him not to worry, and served tea. The next time he called, he tried to get mama to say when we'd leave and where we'd go, but she served tea again, while they chatted about how pretty the water looked and how plainly they could see Catalina Island.

He called a good many times, but it was always the same. Mama didn't give him a chance. One day he rushed out, his ears and stomach full of mama's conversation and tea. He had a wild look in his eye, a paper in his hand. Seeing Flo coming through the gate he thrust the evacuation notice into her hands, saying frantically, "Here, dear, please give this to your mother."

When mama read it, she stared at the ocean for a long time. "Thank you," she said at last, "for a wonderful time."

This turn of affairs called for a family consultation. Six hearts were sad, as we gathered around the driftwood table that evening. We left the decision to daddy. "I've given it thought," he said. "We're going to Hollywood."

"Beachcombers in Hollywood! Can it be possible?" gasped mama.

And so we left Little House.

As we were leaving the sea we said to ourselves: "Farewell Portugese Bend and the little sea lions that sun on the rocks. Farwell Alabone Cove. Don't give your secret to just anybody. Not unless he listens to the song of the sea."

CHAPTER 19

We washed the barnacles off us, found a shop on La Cienega Avenue, a house on Vista Crest Drive, overlooking Cahuenga Pass and the San Fernando Valley. Our truck had been replaced with a Chevrolet sedan which had a heater and radio. We children didn't like it. It was too stuffy. No breezes to play with our braids, and we couldn't see a thing – after the truck, it was very dull transportation.

We were glum as we sped along the cliff road into Hollywood. Farewell, Portuguese Bend and the little sea lions that sun on your rocks. Farewell, Abalone Cove, and your beautiful creatures in their shell houses. Farewell, Paradise Point. Don't give your secrets to "just anybody." Don't let him know what lies hidden in your cave unless he is willing to wait and wait for the tide to go out. Then let him see! Let him squeeze through the narrow opening between the rocks, his ankles splashed by the reluctant tide. Let him enter the dark cavern where water drips from the sea weed growing on the ceiling. Let him sit on the rock over in the corner and listen to the song of the sea. Only here can it be heard. Sometimes a mournful dirge, sometimes a happy chant, according to the Piper Wind's mood. Farewell, farewell!

At Redondo Beach daddy bought us some licorice. We felt better. When we got to Hollywood we stopped at the white building which was to be the shop. All of us explored it. It had been vacated by the photographer, who left dark rooms and plainness. We shook our heads. How could this stark, modern structure be made to look quaint and old enough to hold daddy's beachcomber's beauty? We didn't worry long, however. We caught that look in daddy's eye, a look which in a few months resulted in our shop appearing so old inside and out that even the antique shops on that street seemed new. A moment of nostalgic sadness swept over us as we realized we'd missed the sunset, the first time in many months. Night came quickly in the city. We children hadn't seen our new abode – it was three stories high; slightly run down, and located in a row of houses going up a hill jammed closely to a fine house on one side, a garage on the other. There was no yard at all.

When we reached the front door daddy began to search for the keys–as usual, he completely ransacked himself, and as usual couldn't find them–as usual he apologized disconsolately, saying he'd left them on a rock on the beach that morning to keep them from getting wet. As usual we looked surprised but weren't.

There was only one thing to do, climb through a window. We opened one on the side of the fine house and daddy proceeded to crawl in. At the "one leg in and one out" stage, a whispering voice said, "Are you robbers?" A little girl, with long blond curls, was hanging head first out a window directly opposite.

"No, we're neighbors," daddy answered. "Pretend you're robbers and I'll join you," she said as she scrambled out of the window and took her place in line with the rest of us. Seven slid onto the living room carpet. Mama eased over to the light switch and snapped the button. We gasped.

The room was lovely. Not coldly modern and unattractive as we had imagined, but mountainy and charming. From the windows at the west end we saw the lights of the valley twinkling like stars and heard the wind in the eucalyptus trees sighing like the sea.

When there was a roaring fire blazing in the fireplace, daddy turned his attention to our small robber aspirant companion.

"Would you like to tell us your name?" he asked.

"I'm Pattie Macquarrie," she answered, "and you, you are my friends" – and she threw her arms around The Ba – what a welcome to Hollywood. Seven of us toasted marshmallows around the fireplace that night and seven of us drank hot chocolate. Suddenly the thrill and joy of Little House was in that room. It was a miracle, and the miracle's name was Pattie.

CHAPTER 20

Soon afterward daddy brought home the princess, Princess Olga Paw Paw, an Osage Indian from Oklahoma. He found her peering into the shop. She had imagination. She stayed at our house during the war years, keeping us happy while mama helped daddy. She had the most beautiful long braids and beaded Indian costumes.

She walked so softly – mama said she had real dignity. She taught us how to make Indian dolls from chamois skin, and squaw bread. The latter is easy and dee-licious cooked outside over an open fire.

Sift 2 cups flour, add 1 teaspoon of lard, melted, 1½ cups of cold water. Roll out thin, cut into squares, punch holes in squares of dough and drop into hot fat. Let both sides get golden brown – before eating. You'll simply love squaw bread.

Daddy's first big job was to make the shop look "Come Hitherish" enough to get some customers. There were lookers right off. One little man seemed positively angry that he couldn't understand it. "But vy', vy'," he shouted, "do you do this? Vy' do you stick the top end of a bottle into a cork and use it for a glass, beside charge a dollar and a half for it?" Lookers such as this one made daddy wonder if the whole thing was a mistake.

A little man with a soft voice and a French accent came in. He poked around the beauty lying everywhere. Once in a while he stopped and stared, murmuring, "Hmmmmmm! Interesting!"

Soon he began to beachcomb in earnest, feverishly piling together shells, driftwood, old pieces of iron. He said, "I'd like some fish net, please – this and this and that and this." Daddy got excited – a real, customer, a buying one. Measuring used fish net is always the wildest thing. Daddy used the "from nose to fingertip" method. As he began to throw the net out from his nose arm's length, some of it caught on his sweater button. He attempted to unfasten it but as he dropped the net to the floor it swirled, catching onto another button and one of his shoe laces. Daddy stared at this unexpected development. He couldn't figure out where to start untangling. He knew exactly how a tuna feels. The little man was fascinated. All this time daddy made small talk as though nothing unusual was going on. Mama was horrified. "We'll have to do something." She laughed embarrassedly. "You see, this is all rather new to us, the fish netty business." "Oh, yes," said the little man, "I see." Together he and mama fished daddy out of the net.

Daddy was quiet and dignified as he got the customer's purchases together, but the little man kept bursting into chuckles. He was Eugene Berman, the famous artist and set designer. He became a good friend. Besides doing some stunning decorating with our sea beauty in Miss Ona Munson's house, he used it to study design and form.

One afternoon two "Dese and Dose" characters came in. They were both small, but one was smaller than the other. This one, shifting a big black cigar from one corner of his mouth to the other said, "We want to get some junk for a jernt." "You've come to the right place," said daddy and began to assemble fishnet, old oars, old chests, fish floats, barnacled anchors, and life preservers. The junk went to enhance the subtle attraction of "Slapsy Maxie's."

Then daddy let himself out. Some "free lance" photographers rented him, along with two big ship's lamps, a sou'wester and an oil skin. "If you'll come along, Cap, be our model and tell us how to arrange these lamps, we'll give you fifty bucks," they enticed. Daddy, a model! Or a nautical adviser for that matter! When he went out of the door he asked in a hoarse whisper, "Which is starboard and which is port?"

When he told us about it later he said he almost rebelled when, at the moment of shooting, the photographers threw a big bucket of water in his face to make him look storm-swept.

Some months later when mama and Aunty Ethel were coming back from a three weeks visit in Oklahoma and mama was getting so lonesome for daddy she was about to die, they got of the train in a little town in Texas and made their way to the news stand. There, staring at them from the front of Facts Magazine, was Daddy, sou'wester, storm-swept face, and all. He was supposed to be a merchant marine braving the dangers of the high seas. In the back of the magazine was a long article about him, or rather about a merchant marine, about his long night vigils, his hardships and heartaches. Mama could understand the heartache part as hers had been aching for daddy for some time. She pressed his picture against her cheek, and the aching was better.

Don Beachcomber was one of our best first customers. He is a Texan with an English accent. That combination is hard to beat in Hollywood, which takes to its heart all Texans and is impressed awfully by an English accent. He had his real name officially changed to Beachcomber for business reasons but was glad to meet the real article in daddy. His food is wonderful and so is his war record. He loves sea things and wears a fragrant gardenia lei, flown in fresh every day from Hawaii.

One day, a short time before Christmas, a young man came in with paper and pencil. He asked the price of a number of things. "I am looking for something different for Sam Goldwyn to send out this year," he said. "This lobster crate filled with these bottle and cork goblets is terrific but I'll have to bring Sam by to pass on it." When Mr. Goldwyn came by and saw the crates among the disheveled nauticality, he sputtered, "Why, it's a marine debacle!" And to this day we don't know whether he uttered a "Goldwynism" or whether he hit the nail right on the head. Anyhow he ordered 550 of them. The wheels of industry began to turn. The glass cutter whom daddy had hired along with his machine began to cut glass like mad. Daddy smoothed the corks, mama stuck the bottle tops in the holes, we children poured hot sealing wax on the bottom. Flo, mama, and I delivered them ourselves in order to save time. Mr. Goldwyn certainly sent present to everybody who was anybody – writers, actors, newspaper columnists. Hedda Hopper and Louella Parson both got some.

We children wouldn't have had any fun at all that Christmas if it hadn't been for Haven MacQuarrie, Pattie's father. Haven, who has the "Noah Webster Says" program on the radio, lays down his dictionary on Christmas Eve and becomes Santa Claus. (This is he only time he puts it down during the year. I think he sleeps with it.) He works as hard at Santa as he does at Noah. Perspiration pops out on his forehead as he plays both parts. In his Santa character, his world famous voice booms out from long white whiskers. One of the nicest things about Haven is his family. Besides Patty, there is Ronnie, his son, and Gladys, his wife. Gladys has a Peter Pan soul. I sat on a cake in her car once; when I apologized for having squashed it, she said, "Cakes taste better squashed," and I believe they do.

When Haven's party was over, Paw Paw took us to our shop. It was twelve o'clock, the lovely, witching hour. A sordid view greeted us. Mama was slitting slumped in a chair, her head resting on a pile of goblets on the table in front of her. Daddy was lying on some fish net, mouth open, snoring gently. What price prosperity!

CHAPTER 21

Then daddy decided to enter the Gift Show to be held at the Biltmore Hotel. The night before it opened, mama and daddy worked until four o'clock in the morning, making a bedroom (bed moved out) at the hotel look like a beachcomber's shack. At last daddy's wares had a proper setting. He and mama hung the last piece of net and started home to bed. They stopped at an all-night restaurant for pan cakes and coffee. A man across the table from them was picking his teeth and cleaning his nails with a little gold nail file (apologies to John Steinbeck). Mama and daddy resented anyone looking so fresh, unsleepy, and aggressive at that time of the morning. "Do you two do janitor work?" he started the conversation. "No," answered mama wearily. "We're beachcombers." He looked distressed for a moment, then "My names Barger. I have pottery heads in the gift show at the Biltmore. I'm on my way down there now."

Daddy and mama sighed and went home to bed.

Noon found our parents on their way downtown again with a bad case of stage fright. Goose pimples increased as they reached the hotel and rose to their floor in the elevator. What if no one came into their display at all? What if they did come in and called it junk? What if? Mama considered going back and not appearing at all. Whose idea was this anyway? How could she and daddy have brought all that debris into the Biltmore Hotel?

They started down the hall which led to their display at the very end. A crowd was standing around the doorway. Bright flashes of light came from within the room. Maybe something was terribly wrong. Maybe there was a fire, with all that net. Daddy gave mama's hand a hard squeeze.

Suddenly they saw a familiar figure. Barger, of heads! He squirmed through the crowd. "You're the Hedleys, aren't you," he said breathlessly. "I got it when I saw your display this morning and remembered the fish net you pulled from your pocket at the restaurant, remember? I'm heads, next door. But why were you so late? You've missed the biggest sale of the year. Macy's has just been here and gone – Macy's. My God! Macy's, that name means a million dollars. The newspapers are making pictures and everything and you, where have you been?

"In bed," answered daddy lamely.

The show lasted four days and our exhibit room was full of buyers all the time. Daddy wrote so many orders, he never did fill them all. On the last day of the show, we children were allowed to go down to see things and celebrate with our parents. Daddy was jubilant. He had finally sold the exhibit itself, to be shipped direct to New York.

We dined in style that night, flushed with success. Soft music floated through the prettily lighted Biltmore Bowl. A waiter hovered attentively over our table. Flo and I had on hats, Bungy and The Ba their prettiest pinafores. What a feast we were going to have. We gave our orders. Chicken, turkey, prime ribs of beef, steak, steak—it was up to The Ba. A soft elfish voice said, "I'll take potato soup!"

CHAPTER 22

Sometimes Little House and what it meant to us spoke clearly in a sunset, a blazing fire, or in the wind sighing in the trees, but all in all the excitement and novelty which was Hollywood kept us occupied. Due to gas rationing we hadn't gone anywhere except one time to the mountains, to get away from it all. We went to Mount Waterman where there was snow. We made some dilly skis out of barrel staves.

As we left the last village in the valley and started up the winding road we were one of a long line. As far as we could see ahead, there were cars; as far as we could see behind, there were cars. All over the mountains were people. "Getting away from it all!" mama groaned. We had fun later, though, when we used our barrel skis. Daddy took the most spills and mama had the most laughs. It was like a pretty movie. Even the snow seemed synthetic, it lay in such even mounds. The bright sweaters and caps were a change from the slacks and shorts of Hollywood.

Coming back that evening, mama told us about the happiest snow afternoon in her life. She was ten years old. Her two older sisters Mab and Ethel, whom mama adored, were keeping her. Grandma had gone to "Missionary Society." Snow fell fast and the flakes were big. The picket fence which enclosed the huge yard was creaking under its heavy white load. Inside the fire in the sitting-room fireplace off the icy parlor was burning cheerily. Ethel made fudge. Malcolm (mama) looked out the window at two old cows. They were standing as close to the fence as they could for shelter.

They were skinny and shivering. Malcolm thought of her old Bossy, cozy and warm in her strawy shed, and two big tears rolled down her cheeks. Mab had a warm and tender heart. She couldn't bear to see little girls cry or cows shiver. "Come on," she said. Ethel, Mab, and Malcolm pulled on their coats, boots, and mittens, warmed blankets by the kitchen stove, and plodded through the deep snow to cover the poor animals. They nudged and pushed them into Bossy's shed, leaving them warm and cozy. The snow really did seem wonderful after that. The girls made snow ice cream, mixing snow with beaten eggs, sugar, vanilla, and coconut. They settled down with Whittier's *Snow Bound.* Mama said she guessed she's never felt rosier unless it was ... Her reminiscences were cut short by the bright neon lights and soft tropical air of Hollywood. That was our first and last trip to the mountains.

We all continually longed for our first love, the sea. The coast, down White Point way, was barricaded and closely guarded. We had just enough gas to go to a stretch of land this side of Ventura, the lonesomest, wildest beach we'd ever laid eyes on. Wind blew sand in our eyes and wouldn't let the fire burn at all. "We'll have to do better than this, if we're going to have any fun," said daddy. "Let's build a house and fireplace," we shouted. All of us scattered, looking for building materials. We were at it again. Now we were to have a home off Point Mugu. Four posts were stuck in the ground. Walls went up, a roof thrown on. In about an hour we had a comfortable "lean to," with three sides closed against the sea gale. We fried potatoes and scrambled eggs. The food tasted better than any we'd had in a long time. There's nothing like a bit of sea salt and sand for seasoning. We couldn't go to bed until the moon came up. About twelve o'clock we saw it slowly rising over the little hills, to paint a golden streak on the waters. In the path of light on the wet sand we saw a human figure moving toward us. Who in the world could it be at this hour of night on this lonely stretch of beach? The figure came closer and closer. We children uttered little squeals and our hair sort of stood on end. It was like a mystery movie. Soon we could see plainly that the figure was a man's and that he carried a gun. Suddenly a voice rang into the night above the roar of the breakers. "Halt, who goes there?" "Hallo," shouted daddy. The figure trudged into the light of our fire. He was a young Coast Guardsman. When he found out we were only campers, he put his gun away, sat down, had some coffee and cookies with us, and spun yarns far into the night. He was awfully good looking. I still remember him. When he had gone we climbed into our sleeping bags, and crawled back into our little house on the soft, soft sand. Was there ever a bed so good as this, close to the earth's own heart? It began to rain gently. "Who cares?" we murmured as we sank into deep, untroubled sleep. We had to go back the next day – "back to the old Hollywood hag," said daddy. "I don't know," answered mama dreamily. "She's sort of a hag with a heart." The trip had done mama good.

There's been so much written about Hollywood, most of it bad, but I think it's one of the nicest places in the world.

There are irritating things about Hollywood, of course. Murders are committed across the alley from you, you can't see anything outside at previews any more for the mob of cops (you go to a meeting for aid to some starving country or other and begin to feel that you're sitting in on a Communistic gathering; you go to a meeting for aid to some other starving country or other and begin to feel that Hitler himself might put in an appearance). But those things fade into insignificance before the wonderful atmosphere of Hollywood. Where else is effort so rewarded? Where else is there such freedom of expression? Where else could a composer walk down the street, his hands busily engaged in playing an imaginary piano, and have people only move over to give him room with the remark, "He's writing a new piece – I guess!" Where else could a writer sit on the curb scratching his head, his pencil poised for action, while people tiptoe around him with a Shh!? Where else could people with such hard faces have such soft hearts?

Here I must say a few words about war conditions in Hollywood. Aside from the thing which never leaves anyone when there's a war, the suffering he does with those suffering, the dying he does with those dying, aside from this thing which all of us carry in our hearts when there's a war, we wouldn't have known there was one. It sometimes nauseated me when I shopped for groceries to see fattish women fighting over hunks of meat when there was always plenty of fruits and vegetables.

And so, loving Hollywood as we did, we decided to leave it.

CHAPTER 23

The way we reached this decision is a long story.

Soul-shaking events made every day an historical adventure. President Roosevelt died. A world was sad. The war with Germany ended. A world could barely breathe again.

Flo Ann was in her last year in high school. Everything was running smoothly at the shop. Daddy had two telephones, orders were coming in regularly, decorating jobs were numerous, and the movies were making nautical and South Seas pictures.

One night at dinner daddy rubbed his hands together, looked around the table at his little family (that kind of a look, you know), and to our surprise said, "Well, this is more like it; this is a far cry from Little House, isn't it?" Our surprise was caused by the implication in his tone that this was better than our life there which was perfect. Mama looked shocked. "Have you ever considered," she said icily, "that a vehicle running smoothly sometimes makes a rut?"

Daddy looked shocked. We children were silent.

Shortly after this, our house on the hill in which we lived was sold. We'd have to move again! Daddy came home one day, and excitedly gathered us all into the car to go see the house which he was about to buy. It was near the shop, near Hollywood, near Beverly Hills, near theatres, near Saks, near schools, had a lovely patio, was beautifully, even luxuriously furnished, and had an electric dishwasher! It was oh, ever so convenient, we kept telling ourselves as we wandered disconsolately around the rooms and the grounds. Daddy was enthusiastic as he pointed out its special features. Mama was just quiet. Flo said, "I wonder if they've open up White Point yet?"

We had dinner with mama and daddy at the Players that evening and afterward went over to Paul Hesse's studio to perk up his deck room which daddy had decorated. Paul Hesse photographs movie stars for the fronts of magazines. He is a soft-spoken gentleman, hunts wild pigs on Catalina Island, and has a beautiful view. However, as we stood looking out from Sunset Boulevard at the twinkling lights of Los Angeles, we could see only blue water, white sails, and a little seal on a rock.

When we got to our house we built a fire, using driftwood. Soon the blaze was colored glory. "Shall we toast marshmallows?" said Bungy.

"Let's not, tonight," objected mama. We could hear the radio across the way. It was drowning out the music of the wind. Daddy got up from his chair in front of the fire and walked to the window overlooking the valley. He stood there, hands in his pockets, and stared. "Just think," I said, "an electric dishwasher." Ba, lying on her stomach, chin in her hands, piped up, "Beowulf and Beethoven used to lick our woody plates clean."

At his mama gave a half sob and a half laugh. It didn't take daddy long to cross the room to her side. They both looked at the fire a long time. Daddy cleared his throat, took a deep breath, and said, "Boys (he always called us that, I can't imagine why), I'm afraid I was beginning to yaw but I'm seeing my course clearly tonight. For some time now, I've been thinking of your future only in terms of money and of what the world considers a high standard of living." He gestured rather grandly. "I see I have done you a grave injustice.

95

I have under-rated your characters. Now," he looked earnestly in each of our faces, "let's go back to the sea!"

The hubbub in that room drowned out even the radio across the way. We tumbled daddy onto the floor and all of us jumped on top of him, rolling him over and over around the room. "Oh, daddy, daddy, can we, can we?" we all shouted at once. When we were worn out with our tumbling match, we looked around for mama. She was busily toasting marshmallows. "The Heavenly Satisfaction" look was on her face.

A few weeks later, when night had lighted the stars, daddy rose from the dinner table, snuffed out the candles, and said, "Now, I have a present for you. Grab your sleeping bags. Let's go." Pandemonium, as we flew to our rooms, slipped into jeans, tucked our sleeping bags under our arms and scrambled into the car. Away we went, past Redondo, past Palos Verdes, past Portuguese Bend, past Abalone Cove. Here was White Point! We turned sharply, passed the spot where Little House used to nestle, coasted down the hill and came to a big wooden gate. Above it, shining faintly in the moonlight, was a driftwood sign on which was spelled out in brown rope, "Hedley's Trade Winds Cove." As we spilled out of the car daddy said, "This, my beachcombers, is your new home." We entered the gate shyly, reverently. There was only the sound of the sea pushing back and forth with signs of contentment.

We felt a little sad kind of happiness like when the war was over. We looked up at the moon as it swam silverly above wisps of cloud. We stared fascinatedly at the lacy patterns of the palms against the sky. Flo Ann crumpled and sat right down on the ground. "I'm sorry," she said, in a muffled voice, "this is all I can take tonight. 'My cup runneth over.' Let's build a fire and go to bed in front of the fireplace. We'll explore tomorrow." Soon fire roared up the chimney (blessed driftwood). A gentle breeze stirred the white and gold blossoms of the copa de oro vine over our heads. A night bird screamed. The sea kept sighing contentedly. We lay in our sleeping bags wide awake and dreamed.

Our cove is magic. A bit of heaven between a high hill and the sea.

"The sea sighed contendely. We lay in our sleeping bags wide awake and dreamed. 'Our cove is magic...a bit of heaven between a high hill and the sea.'"

CHAPTER 24

You know, by now, that our cove is something felt and seen, too; the something seen has a history. It was part of a land grant by Governor Pio Pico to Jose Lareto Sepulveda and Juan Sepulveda, brothers. Of one of their descendants and of our cove, a *Los Angeles Times* correspondent wrote in the September 26, 1926, issue of the paper, "Don Roman Sepulveda is the lone horseman of San Pedro. Once his family owned much of the land now in the town, and he rode over it on horseback, monarch of all he surveyed, and Don Roman still rides horseback, still wears his fine Spanish sombrero, still looks and acts the haughty Don, as if defying time, changeless in the midst of swift perpetual change. A striking figure of old romance on the skyline of the city just awakening like a mighty giant to its new romance of achievement and progress. Fifty years ago Don Roman set out a row of palm trees along the edge of the beach at White Point. Today those trees are the evidence of how one man's effort to beautify the world may survive." Don Roman died a number of years ago, but the yearning in a man's heart to beautify the world still lives. That's the thing felt. He had descendants, too.

The one we know best is Louie, who looks like any other Californian. You'd think he came from Kansas or Iowa. However, one time I caught him looking out to sea. He had changed. He looked thrilling somehow. I like to think that his veneer is only skin deep and underneath still lives the fiery, adventurous spirit of the early Spanish explorer. (Goodness, I am getting as bad as mama.)

When we awoke in Don Roman's cove next morning, we saw sea gulls fluttering like bits of torn paper around a fishing boat headed into the harbor, we saw White Point and the cliff where daddy had hung on for dear life and had learned that Shakespeare was right. We saw the little pier running out into the bay where mama had lost her conventions; but most of all, looking further, we saw ourselves lying in the sun, swimming off the rocks, reading under the shade of the big palms, dancing on the terrazzo dance floor left over from the cove's country club days; but we woke again when daddy said, "All right, boys, up and at 'em! We're going to bring everything down from Hollywood, you know – lock, stock, and barrel. I'm anxious to move the shop from La Cienega as we've filled up the building there and are spilling over into the alley. Why, I heard a lady decorator refer to our starfishes, old shoes, big logs, and dead sharks as 'junk cluttering up the driveway.'" To our dismay we saw a look in daddy's eye, a look which resulted in our working from early morning till late at night all summer.

Sometimes we rebelled. "I always thought beachcombers led a sort of lolly life, lolling around under some bough a la Omar Khayyam," our spokesman Flo Ann said. "Hedley beachcombers are different," said daddy. We certainly were. We would have put ants to shame.

By the time we children started to school in September, we had dug a well, put in a water system, built a shop, and planted a house. (It's still sprouting.) We did this with sea drift. "You can count the times we went to the lumber yard on the fingers of one hand," says daddy proudly.

We slept outside on cots until the bedrooms were built. We hated to go inside. We didn't until the rains came. All of us got so brown, we looked like South Sea Islanders. We felt as though we'd like to live under the sky forever.

One morning we saw Flo Ann carrying her cot from under the trees in front of the fireplace to put it on the rock on the beach. "What are you doing?" shouted daddy. "I'm moving closer to the sea," she yelled back. "It's too stuffy out here."

We cooked on the barbecue. I figured a way to make biscuits without an oven. I placed them on a pancake griddle, covered them with a heavy iron skillet (which I had found on the beach, handleless), and pushed them to the back of the iron plate on top of the barbecue, where it wasn't too hot. They were as good as Carrie's, almost.

And so, as mama says, either our house is the worst thing in the world or else what she has always wanted. One of its worst features is it's leaky. Still, that has its advantages. We play a game about it. Various members of the family at various times win various things, such as ice cream sodas, movie tickets, and new tennis balls. It's a funny thing, but there are two kinds of people who come to our house, those who see the cracks in the shingle roof and ask, "What do you do when it rains?" And those who see the cracks in the roof and don't ask. Our game is to bet on which ones will and which ones won't. Daddy's answer is always the same, given in his most professorial manner, "Oh, we just let it rain!"

The best features of our house are: It's made of blessed driftwood, it doesn't shut out the outside too much, and it doesn't interfere with our joy of living. We like the fireplace made from the hood of a blacksmith's forge; the stained glass window through which we have the Red Sea, as well as a Pacific one; the "welcome" carved on the lower step leading to the deck living room, the twisted white tree daddy used as a banister; and the bathroom with driftwood at either end of the tub, as towel racks. Green ivy, growing in wooden tubs, curls up and around the branches. When we have especially luscious guests, like Alice Armer, we add gardenias and hibiscus to the limbs. Alice has blond hair and a Greek goddess figure. Daddy remembers that one time when she was a guest at our house in Seminole, Oklahoma, she got eleven orchids from different suitors. Now she's married to Lee Armer, an oil man, and lives in Fort Worth, Texas. Their son calls her "motha." It seems incongruous somehow.

To get back to the house and to sum it up, it was probably done best for us by daddy's cowboy uncle, Eli, who stands only five feet in his high-heel boots and wears a huge Stetson hat. He said, "Wal', this is the dangdest thing I ever see!"

CHAPTER 25

For some time life at Trade Winds Cove has run on a fairly even keel, that is, judged by Hedley standards. Of course this business of beachcombing is always exciting and every day an adventure. Sometimes the adventure is purely mental. Like the feeling the flight of a bird in the gray dawn gives you. Like the loneliness and loveliness of a ship's whistle heard while reading in bed on a night when the fog's fingers are pushing against the window pane.

Sometimes the adventure can be real, like the rainy day the old tug boat *Listo* finally gave up and sank on our beach, giving us ship's lamps, life preservers, and ship's bells. She was the oldest tug in the Los Angeles harbor.

I dare say, an ordinary observer might scratch his head at some of our goings-on, but none of our friends are ordinary. There's Ramon, for instance. Ramon always understands. He is a Basque from the Pyrenees who can write beautiful words, cook rabbits in wine, and dance the tango, but best of all, no matter what we do, he understands. Once he told us we had done a wonderful thing for him. "I always thought I was a little off," he said. "Until I met all of you – now I don't know!" Ramon is one of the kindest persons we know. We love the way he says, "She's beautiful, isn't it?" and concerning the French harp, which we call harmonica, "I like philharmonica music." In fact, we love him.

Then there's the pirate. His name is Don Dickerman. He's had five wives and many night clubs in New York City. He worked for daddy for a while. Now he has the Castaway Club in Balboa. We went there for dinner the other night. The pirate showed us two little leaves his sister-in-law had brought him from Brazil. A worm had worked beautiful lacy patterns on them. "Did you ever see anything so beautiful, Cap? Huh, did you?" he asked ecstatically. He has a wonderful sense of values. This business of beachcombing creates some interesting customers. There's Joseph Platt. His chauffeur brings him to go beachcombing with daddy. He calls himself an industrial designer, but to us he's a fine artist, not only in creating but in knowing how to live. Behind his back we call him the Presence, not because he's impressive at all but because somehow when he enters a room all else pales before his humble dominion.

There's Miss Helen Winslow. She is gift buyer for Carson, Pirie, Scott in Chicago. The reason we children like her is because she treats us like we're "the children." You know, sort of like we're a conglomeration of child, but Miss Winslow deals with us individually, and that's the way we like it. Mama loves her because she has the right idea about words. "For instance," we heard her tell mama, "take the word *misled*. I called it *mizled* when I was a child. I was so shocked when I found out it was *misled*." Daddy loves her because she has soft blue eyes, soft blond hair touched with gray, owns a little island in Canada, and said to him concerning his huge war surplus, L.C.I. boat, which graces our beach and which daddy bought hoping to sell it and make some money, "Why don't you sell it to Marshall Field's to plant?"

There are Mr. and Mrs. Gary Cooper who came for driftwood for their ski lodge in Aspen, Colorado. The first time mama served coffee to Gary she was so excited, she spilled the sugar. The way he dashed to her rescue, the shy way he put her at ease, forever endeared him to mama. Gary's ability as an actor, is his ability to realize that he can't act. He's himself and that's worth paying to see any day. One of his greatest successes is Mrs. Cooper.

There are Mr. and Mrs. Gibbons. Mr. Gibbons writes Western movies and Mrs. Gibbons designs beautiful dresses under the name of "Irene." Mr. Gibbons is one of the few people we know who has not lost he art of conversation. He doesn't say words, he says ideas. In order to talk with him you have to think. You can't listen to the radio at the same time. Irene is boyish, having been brought up on a ranch in Montana, and completely lovely inside and out.

There's Ona Munson, wife of our good friend, Eugene Berman. He uses her as a model for his paintings, mostly in his imagination, but as a dream or as a reality Ona's beautiful.

One of our nicest customer friends is Chief Pua Kealoha. He is a champion, being the only swimmer to top Johnny Wiessmuller at the backhand stroke. Pua was once thin and handsome; now he is fat but still handsome. He is the best diver we've ever seen. Always brings up lobsters and "abs" (a pet name for abalones after you get used to them).

When Pua appears at the front door, we drop everything and fit our plans in with his. There's something about him as he stands there smiling, that makes us know that this is the thing to do. Call it intuition, call it a sixth sense, we know its right to cease all activity immediately and line up with Pua. What is time, what is industry, what is tomorrow in the face of Pua's ever present now? Everything slows down. We laugh, we sing, we even dance as we shovel dirt from the pit where we're going to cook the little pig that Pua has brought. When the hole has been dug about four feet across and four feet deep we light a fire inside it; using eucalyptus or oak tree wood. We let this burn down to coals; then place lava stones or holey beach rocks (the only kind that won't pop when heated) around over the coals. We cover the rocks with glossy green Ti leaves that Pua gets from his native Hawaii (you can use banana leaves or even grape), making a thick bed for the little pig to lie on. We stuff him with hot rocks, tie his feet together, carry him on a long pole and dump him gently in the pit. Around him go hunks of fish, pieces of chicken, and sweet yams wrapped in Ti leaves (or banana or grape). We cover him quickly with wet white sacks (the kind you use for cup towels), throw on more Ti leaves (or banana or grape), gunny sacks, a few more hot stones, then all of us begin to shovel dirt frantically and throw it on top. I don't know what there is about frantic shoveling that makes the Luau a success but undoubtedly it does. You must act as though you think the pig is going to get up and run away.

For three hours we relax. We swim, we listen to Pau tell tales of old Hawaii, of how happy the people were, and how safe. We listen to him sing softly his people's religious law, comparable to our "Do unto others as you would have them do unto you," and to his chanting wildly "The Hawaiian War Chant," which is really a love song. When Pua gives the signal, we rush to the pit with our shovels. This time we dig carefully. All we can see at first is a cloud of steam. Stomach warming fragrances float through the air: roast pig, baked yams, roast chicken, and fish. We lift this heavenly feast onto a big wooden platter and carry it to the La Haulla mat. We sit around it cross-legged on other mats. We eat off Tahitian pearl shells, with our fingers, dipping poi from a big bowl. Pua makes his own poi from Taro root he gets from the islands. Poi looks like wallpaper paste but tastes like ambrosia, if you're the type.

For hours, we eat, we laugh, we sing. At last the moon rises over White Point, giving us dreams and taking them away, for this is Pua's signal for departure. He must make his appearance soon, singing and dancing with his orchestra at the Lei Lani Restaurant, but Pua has given us a beautiful gift, the memory of a happy, happy day.

Gene and Ina Autrey are very nice people. Gene talks the way he does in his western movies, but Ina uses good grammar, having taught school in Oklahoma. He likes biscuits and gravy and does sleight-of-hand tricks. He tosses a fifty-cent piece wrapped in a handkerchief up to the ceiling. The latter comes down while the former stays right there. I haven't figured that one out, but it may have something to do with chewing gum which Gene keeps always handy.

Our family met the Autreys at Bradford Browne's house. Brad is a tall, lanky "down easter" born in North Adams, Massachusetts, in the Berkshire Hills. He loves writing cowboy songs and has by the thousands. None of us can ask for anything better than for Brad to sit stiffly at his grand piano, with his perpetually worried face, and sing Western songs with his nasally Eastern accent. Brad managed Gene for a while and I must say he managed very well as he managed to get the name of a town in Oklahoma changed from Berwyn to Gene Autrey. It took the sanction of the Post Office department and the Santa Fe Railroad to do this. Brad was pretty excited over it, as thirty thousand people came in for the celebration, including notables such as Governor Phillips, Dr. Claude Chambers, and a bunch of Indians who pitched their wigwams nearby; but Gene took these events in his stride, having a most even disposition. He just kept chewing gum.

Gene likes and sings Brad's "Git Along Little Pony" best but we like his "Cowboy Without a Guitar."

It goes –

One day in Wyomin' I met an old man,
For years he'd been searchin' for gold
He told me a story as strange as could be –
And this was the story he told.

I have traveled this mighty world over,
From Cheyenne to old Zanzibar.

107

'Twas in Texas that I saw the strangest of sights,

A COWBOY WITHOUT A GUITAR.

He was ridin' a bucking young bronco,

Who tossed him about near and far.

I had to look twice to be sure that I saw

A COWBOY WITHOUT A GUITAR.

CHORUS:

Oh, sing me a song of the West, Mister Cowboy,

Yippi i, yippy ay, get along little stray.

Oh, sing me a song of the West, Mister Cowboy,

And then I'll be off on my way.

I've seen coyotes that howl in the daytime

And a monkey that smoked a cigar,

But I ain't been the same since the day that I saw

A COWBOY WITHOUT A GUITAR.

I thrill at the sight of Niag'ra

My heart jumps at each movie star,

But the one thrill I got that I'll never forget

WAS A COWBOY WITHOUT A GUITAR.

He was brandin' a steer in Montana,

In his hand was a smokin' red bar,

At first I was doubtful, but folks, there he was,

A COWBOY WITHOUT A GUITAR.

CHORUS:

Oh, sing me a song of the West, Mister Cowboy,

Yippi i, yippy ay, git along little stray.

Oh, sing me a song of the West, Mister Cowboy,

And then I'll be off on my way.

I've seen princes and kings in pajamas,

And rustlers in feather and tar,

But I'm ready to die now that I have beheld

A COWBOY WITHOUT A GUITAR.

Customer friend Harold Marconda has the Coral Reef in the great Farmer's Market. Daddy built his first building for him. It was an authentic Los Angeles Tahitian shack. The only trouble was, when it rained, Harold and his clerks were too busy sweeping water out the doors and emptying water out of beer mugs and vases to make any sales. Now his South Seas shop is in a New England red barn which is dry, if not appropriate. Harold is the owner of a mynah bird. He heartily recommends mynahs to anyone whose business is bad. This little black bird with its Hallowe'en candy corn bill, comes from India and talks sometimes. He draws crowds of people around his cage and screeches when they mis-pronounce his name, which is Jose. He always says, "Are you a Tough Guy?" "Hello, Mr. Bugsby," and is the originator of the "wolf call." One day he said all kinds of things.

"Where did you get that silly hat, lady?" "Why don't you buy something, you suckers?" and "Hello, you old crow." Harold was about to call the museum to tell them of his wonderful find when

Ella, his clerk, nudged him with her elbow and said, "That's Edgar Bergen in front of the cage."

Jose eats like a maharajah. Orange juice and mashed hard boiled egg yolk for breakfast, avocado for lunch, banana for dinner.

The great Farmer's Market makes its greatest appeal to tourists and to stomachs. It's the perfect place for out-of-town shopping wives to leave husbands. They wander around all day, keeping out of mischief, getting fuller and fuller.

There are the Vanderlips. Mr. Kelvin Vanderlip heads the Palos Verdes Corporation, a real estate development in these hills. Mrs. Vanderlip, a charming Norwegian, believes in inviting children to dinner along with their parents. Of course daddy is awfully unhappy about the club house they built at Portuguese Point, but that is because he can't forget how it used to be there. The dusty, winding road, bright in the sunlight, the daisies which grew on either side, swaying gracefully before the sea wind, the black wharf, crumbling with age, where he could tie his boat, and most of all the wailing of the many voices. Only our family and a few Naamite friends know of this. One day, when we were beachcombing at Portuguese Bend, mama stooped over to tie her shoe. She stayed bent over for so long a time, we began to wonder. When she raised herself to standing position she listened for a moment, a wild expression on her face, then quickly went back down again. Her actions were too peculiar to uninvestigated. Five us came running from our respective places on the beach. Mama murmured loudly, "Shhhhhh!" "What is it mama?" "The wailing of voices," said mama hollowly, from her upside down position. "I expect it comes from the ones who have lived and loved the sea and been buried in her," she continued dramatically. "What on earth!" we said as we followed mama's suit, head down to shoes. Soon we too were immobile. We too heard it. An "Aouuoooooo" like human voices, moaning and weeping. We found that here was the only place on the beach where it could be heard. We marked the spot with our secret marker which is still there today. The reason we call our friends who have heard it, Naamites, is because, they like Naaman were not too proud; he, to bathe seven times in a dirty river, they to go upside down on the beach to listen for voices. Daddy also found some whale's teeth. He made salt and pepper shakers out of them. Mama couldn't get over them as they were so cute and solid ivory.

We children are not unhappy about he club, however, as we love the swimming pool and Mr. Neil Petree's comfortable Barker Bros. furniture. The big house where the Vanderlips live looks like an Italian villa and is called The Villetta. The Frank Vanderlips, Kelvin's mama and papa, traveled, bringing back many treasures from many lands. I love Mrs. Kelvin Vanderlip for letting the house stay as it was. It's worn enough to be lovely and only occasionally have a beautiful table's legs been cut off to make it more "functional."

The dining room is best with its long, long table, its huge sideboard filled with old silver, and its intriguing Austrian wine machine. This has an iron base with an iron rod going up out of it. Attached to this is a circular glass tube. The wine bottle is placed in a funnel at the top and the wine runs down, red and beguiling, to the bottom of the tube where there is a ball-bearing contraption against which you press your glass to fill it. It's fun to work it, and

Mrs. Vanderlip lets you, as long as you can get somebody to drink its contents, which usually isn't hard.

It's easy to run into famous people at the Vanderlips, such as Katherine Hepburn, Greta Garbo, Ethel Barrymore, Cole Porter, and the Charles Laughtons. Mrs. Charles Laughton, Elsa Lanchester, works, that is plays, at the Turnabout, in Hollywood. This theater is called that because in the middle of the program the audience gets up and turns about, viewing the other end. Daddy thinks the only end which amounts to anything is the one which shows Elsa, as he thinks she's the funniest thing in town. She gave Kelvin a funny present all right – a group of pictures of her feet, tired, gay, tipsy, and every which way.

My favorite among the Vanderlips is Charlotte Vanderlip Conway, Kelvin's sister, who teaches anthropology at Palos Verdes College. Her outside is fashioned after the pattern of a perfect lady but her inside is considerably rebellious against "perfect lady standards." She has a passionate interest in the un-white man of the world, and is firmly convinced that civilization has been his downfall. However, she is not opinionated and teaches us a great deal through her lovely teachableness.

Also it's easy to run into peacocks on this ranch, as they roam wild and free all over the place. One hot sunny day, I was sketching the old red barn, which everybody always sketches, when close by me, with a tremendous flutter, rose this bird of many colors. He alighted a few feet away, gave a weird cry, and stood quietly looking at me. I smiled, not being able to speak his language. We sat that way, peacock and I, for over an hour, he cocking his head, surely retaining in his way impressions of beauty from his peacock world, as I was retaining, in my way, impressions of beauty from an old red barn with yellow mustard growing round.

Daddy has forgiven Mr. Vanderlip for making Portuguese Bend so modern since he was thoughtful enough to plant peacocks on the place.

Eastern customer friends who love driftwood are Mr. and Mrs. Joffee. Mr. Joffee photographs for *Vogue,* and has something to do with advertising. He tells funny stories. We thought his funniest one was about the model who worked years aspiring to be the glamour of Tabu and finally made it. After five times posing for that luscious liquid, she was happy in her great success and went back to her small town, well satisfied.

Mrs. Joffee is the chicquest thing. Their New York apartment is filled with driftwood lamps, tables, and chairs, designed and made by Mr. Joffee in his living room. Mrs. Joffee wishes they had a work shop when she moves hammers and saws off of tables before serving coffee to guests. Some pieces of driftwood they get from daddy. Others they get by themselves from the Point at Nantucket. Once they spent twelve hours trying to dislodge a big stump from the sands there.

They took a truck with two husky helpers, a jeep, and their young son who gleefully enjoyed the gory procedure of unearthing the wood.

They found upon arrival in the morning that they'd made a mistake about the time of tide. Instead of low, it was high.

They picnicked, played bridge with the two husky helpers, waded and built castles in the sand. They talked over and over again what they'd do with the big beautiful driftwood stump. Kuniyoshi was going to help them make it.

When the tide was low enough to latch one end of a chain on to it, they did. One of the two husky helpers got into the jeep they'd rented for the day and backed bravely toward the stump. Down, down he went into the soft, soft sand. Everybody worked hard dislodging the jeep. Young son was hilarious.

When the jeep was free, one of the husky helpers latched it on to the other end of the chain, and he and the jeep pulled hard. The stump wouldn't budge. Mr. Joffee, Mrs. Joffee, the other husky helper and young son pushed with all their might. Again the stump wouldn't budge. Mrs. Joffee took husky helper's place at the wheel. Husky helper pushed along with the others, and finally the old stump heaved itself out of the sand and allowed itself to be dragged bit by bit to a safe dry place. Mrs. Joffee's feet were calloused for weeks afterward as she was still barefooted when she took the wheel.

They threw themselves pantingly on the sand to rest and triumphantly regard their future something or other. Suddenly Mr. Joffee, who is slightly temperamental, being such a fine artist at his work, jumped up and began tearing his hair. "The piece is ugly," he screamed. "We can't use it. Look at it. All arms and legs underneath where it was buried. We can't use that thing." The husky helpers drove off in disgust. Mr. and Mrs. Joffee didn't speak all the way home, but young son did. He talked of his wonderful outing.

Daddy makes Mr. Joffee a good price on driftwood since he knows and loves it and works so hard to get it.

We have awfully good times with friend and customer Harry Lachman. Harry has the Patio Shop in Beverly Hills. It's filled with ideas. One of the cutest of these is an old-fashioned potty planted with ivy and made into a lamp with a bright red shade. Daddy sings, "Ohoo the Patio's potties are potted." I think he's jealous because he didn't think of planting potties!

Tai is a beautiful Chinese woman who looks like an artificial flower but smells like a real one. She gives dinner parties for celebrities at which she serves eggs a hundred years old.

Harry and Tai know everyone in Beverly Hills. Their guest book reads like "Who's Who of the World." It lies on a podium near the front door, and you have to be a very important person before you're asked to sign it. In fact, you practically have to have been mentioned in Louella Parsons' column. They introduce us to the nicest people such as the Edward Robinsons. The Robinsons have the loveliest house, filled with a collection of paintings mostly by the French impressionists.

Harry wears the red ribbon of the Legion of Honor proudly, but all the same he seems sad. Still, I'd rather be sad with Harry than happy with others I know.

And there's our friend Madame Stravinsky, wife of Igor. She's my ideal. Her soft, fair hair is parted in the middle and swirls back over lovely ears. Her eyes are enchanting. They're violet sometimes and hold the romance, the mystery, and yes, the misery of Russia. Her voice sounds like the low notes on a flute.

As busy as she is, she remembers four beachcomber girls with presents and Russian goodies.

There's Gladys Cooper. She is a great actress but talks most about gardening. She has interesting grown children and brings them to the Cove with her. Her son, John Buckmaster, played in *The Importance of Being Earnest.* They all speak with the nicest British accents. We love the way they say "Buckmaster." Miss Cooper is witty and clever, but if she thinks she's said anything to hurt you she's very sorry. She is gracious and charming and seems more a "lady" than an "actress" but really is both.

CHAPTER 26

Daddy's helpers are also understanding.

There's Alfred, a slender, wiry little man, hard as nails. His hair shows a few streaks of gray. He speaks with a German accent. He went to sea in a windjammer at the age of twelve. He puts ships into bottles for daddy. Alfred can spin yarns. When he talks he loses all sense of time, as do we when we listen. Mama and daddy are forever breaking in to want Alfred to do something or us to go to bed. The yarn we love best is about his adventures off Helgoland. He was shipwrecked, clinging to pieces of wood in the icy water for two weeks (sometimes it was three weeks, and once after several bottles of beer it was a month.) He ate potatoes from his ship's galley larder when they drifted by close enough for him to grab them. When he comes to the part about saying his prayer – "Now I lay me down to sleep" every night, with his head pillowed on a slimy piece of wood, the rest of him stiff in the icy waters, we cry, but are always made happy immediately because of his rescue by a herring lugger.

There's Beulah, she's a sprite. Mama says her thin, dignified body and plain face are to fool people and make it more exciting when they discover her impish insides. She is hardly ever with us although her body goes around doing things for daddy: making lampshades, painting sea captains on old jugs, and even scrubbing the shop. Sometimes she takes us to her world of artistic perception, and there we love to be. Once I told mama she reminded me of Gainsborough's "Blue Boy." I asked mama if that was awfully silly. After all, Beulah has seen a good many birthday celebrations. She said, "No, there is something about Beulah's eyes, so clear, so deep, and her head so fine, so proud."

There's Edna, our sea-weed artist. She it was who discovered the art of pickling ocean flowers so they could keep their color and not get smelly. She did this in her apartment bathtub. She always had trouble with landladies. Edna is a good beachcomber and a courageous lady.

Wally is our most unforgettable character. He takes a positive stand against everything. When daddy says in the morning, "Now, boys, let's get on the line and get some stuff out," Wally looks knowing and leaves soon afterward to trudge for hours on the beach. When someone in the shop said, "A boy should know a girl a long time before marrying her," Wally looked knowing again. In a few days he brought us Doris. He had met her one evening, proposed, married her the next day. Not only that but he had taken her to Reno for the wedding. But Wally works like a Trojan when he wants to.

There are Mr. Doi and Mr. Tanaka. Mr. Doi had a café in San Pedro before he was sent to a relocation center, so he only knows how to cook hamburgers and hot dogs, but Mr. Tanaka showed us how to make sukiyaki, how to boil snails in sea water, how to pick the meat out with tooth picks, and how to eat with chop sticks. The only thing hard about sukiyaki is, you're supposed to cook one portion at a time. That's why the Japanese people have sukiyaki tables with a built-in stove so the food can be assembled right there. We fudge, however, make several portions at once, and it's still delicious.

Get together a few pieces of beef suet, sirloin steak, sliced thin, one Bermuda onion, chopped green onions and celery, fresh or canned mushrooms, sliced, one cake Tofu (soy bean curd).

Begin by frying suet in skillet, add meat, onions, celery, cover with three-fourths of cooking sauce, let simmer fifteen minutes, stir occasionally with chop sticks (this gives authenticity), add Tofu (in chunks), mushrooms, and rest of sauce. The recipe for sauce is: one-half cup sake sauce (rice wine), one-fourth cup soy sauce, one-fourth cup meat broth, one tablespoon sugar.

Inhale sukiyaki with chop sticks.

Besides giving us recipes, Mr. Doi and Mr. Tanaka work for daddy.

There's John, who is long and lanky and just our age. He is a typical rancher. He talks for hours about how much fun it is to trudge mud to feed cows, or to refertilize ground. We retaliate with salty yarns about emptying lobster pots or sailing a cat boat. John is practical. It is sometimes hard for him to adjust himself to us.

He lives in Hollywood, but stays at the cove some nights. One morning at breakfast Bungy held up a dollar, saying, "See what the horse fairy brought me last night?" "The what?" questioned John amazedly. "The horse fairy," Bungy repeated. "I want a horse, horses cost money, the horse fairy knows it so every once in a while she brings me a dollar." John exploded. "Why doesn't your daddy just come out and give you the dollar ..." He went no further when he saw the horrified expressions on the faces around the table. Mama came to the rescue. "It is hard for John to understand how it is that Bungy will enjoy the horse more if the horse fairy pays for it ..."

She broke off and finished lamely, "just like, well for instance the same way I like pressed flowers." Everybody laughed and rescued the situation that time.

A week later mama got a letter. Inside was a sprig of flat sweet peas – also a card on which was written "From the Pressed Flower Fairy." Mama said, "Our John can go along with a gag."

There is also John Fishersmith. He was born in London, England. His adventurous spirit led him from panning gold to making diving helmets. One summer we met "Around-the-World-Single-Handed" Captain Pigeon and visited him on his little boat, *The Islander.* He gave us wonderful beans cooked in an iron pot on an iron stove. He is a happy man and a buttermilk drinker. On his long voyage by himself, he never had any coffee. Only once, however, did he go to sleep when he was supposed to stay awake. That time his boat intuitively felt her way to the only stretch of sand between a mile-long wall of rocks on either side and beached herself. He has great faith, but no religion. We borrowed the book, *How to Make Your Own Diving Helmet,* from him! Flo, John, and I started with vigor. We cut a hole in one end of a five-gallon paint can and shaped it to fit our shoulders. We slit one side of a rubber hose and pushed it over the metal edge. This made a comfortable padding. We made a window of airplane plexi-glass and bolted it on with a gasket between it and the metal. This window almost got us into trouble as we shaped it in the oven at the same time mama was baking a cake. Flo was watching and became so excited when she saw it melted that she shouted, "It's done, it's done." Mama was outside and came running like mad, thinking it was her baking. When she saw the plexi-glass and a fallen cake she didn't feel kindly toward home-made diving equipment. When the window was set we connected a gas station air hose to a valve at the top. The idea was to pump air through this with a foot tire pump. The day came to try it out. We trekked to the spot which we call our lagoon. The rocks form a small pool where all sorts of beautiful sea creatures thrive. Flo and John went down with varying degrees of success. They kept bobbing up. Our lagoon just wasn't deep enough. No sport here. They decided to go in *Skol* and let each other over the side. The sea was like a lake. There was nothing to fear. When they cast anchor they waved gaily.

John stood up, beat his chest, and uttered Tarzan yells. Flo fitted the helmet carefully over his head, and he slid into the water. Suddenly our attention was diverted from Flo's frantic pumping to a dark movement in the water. Huge dark movement! Bearing down upon them from starboard. Daddy shouted, "A whale!" We saw *Skol* rise straight up as the whale slid past. She miraculously settled in an upright position. But John, what of John! He was under the water somewhere in a whirlpool of motion left by that mammoth passing. We could only wait and watch. Flo was working on the hose. Soon we saw her pull John over the side. Together they unrigged him and rowed quickly to shore. They were both green and wouldn't talk. Later, however, Flo swore that John's first words upon feeling *Skol* beneath his feet were, "I say, that water wasn't a bit cold."

Daddy today points to the diving helmet, hanging provocatively from a nail on the wall of the shop, and says, "You can really use this homemade contraption, you know, but ..." and he lengthens his already long chin, "I'd like to see anyone try it!"

And then there's Bill. Bill has a big truck and hauls driftwood · for daddy. Besides being a gentleman trucker, he is also a gentleman tree doctor, a gentleman adventurer, a gentleman unafraid! Bill stutters when he talks to some people. The day he came to see daddy about a job was a stormy one. Above the howling of the wind, the roar of the sea, and the steady drumming of the rain upon the roof, we heard a tune being played on the old zither that serves as a bell on our front door. Bungy flew to welcome the seeker for shelter. There stood Bill. He looked like a character out of the Buck Rogers funny paper strip. He had on everything the war surplus store had to offer in the way of rain gear. Handy gadgets, such as a flint lighter for an acetylene torch, a direction finder, and a machete hung from his belt. His first words were, "It's sure wwwet out here." Bungy ushered him up the stairs and relieved him of his protection against the weather. Bill settled himself into a comfortable corner by the fire, downed a cup of coffee, drew his knees up under his chin and began to talk. "I've b-been down in Florida d-digging for treasure and d-diving for jewels on sunken v-vessels." Ba's eyes grew big. "I saw a mermaid once," she broke into Bill's raconteuring. Bill stroked his chin, looked at Ba for a while without saying anything, then began to talk again. This time he didn't stutter at all. Bill had done everything, everything that is that would keep him out of the ranks of the employed. Somehow Social Security was anathema to him; only by contract, and on his own would Bill work.

When the rain let up he took us out to show us his truck. As permanent equipment he carried two big ladders, a block and tackle, a cable, a chain saw, a hoist, and an iron cage. When we asked what he used that for he said, "Ah, that's for mountain lions."

Needless to say, Bill was contracted for by daddy that very day. It was a good thing because if Bill hadn't been along we probably wouldn't have got our next load of driftwood at all. We went to Point Conception where ships have been crashing on the rock for years. Here there was treasure for the beachcombers. When we came to the big iron gate that opened onto the road leading down to the sea, we found it didn't open at all. It was locked with three locks.

Daddy would have to see somebody. We went with him to the overseer's house five miles away. He had some keys but he didn't know whether they would unlock the gate or not. Back we dashed. They wouldn't. There was one more chance. The overseer's overseer had some keys. He was in Lompoc shopping. To the village we sped. Eighteen miles around curving roads, got the key, and back again to the big iron gate.

During all this feverish activity Bill sat calmly in his truck reading Dwight Long's *Seven Seas on a Shoestring*. When we came back the second time he stood by the gate. It was open.

The overseer got out, brandishing his keys efficiently. Daddy looked embarrassed. "What happened, Bill?" he asked. "Oh, I had a screw d-driver, so I j-just used it!" answered Bill. He added, "I l-learned how to open l-locks without keys when I was r-rustlin' cattle in Texas."

The overseer cleared his throat vigorously. We all thanked him a shade too effusively, I thought, as he left in the jeep.

Some people think Bill is odd with his shock of uncombed gray hair, his fifteen-year-old Harris tweed coat, his tie worn as splicing for his suspenders instead of around his neck, but Bill has something that they haven't got and that is a look in his eye that will never grow old.

CHAPTER 27

We could almost live on what we catch from the sea. However, our favorite foods are lobsters and grunions. The west coast variety of lobster is little more than a crawdad, but oh, so tender and delicious! We run pots every evening, rowing out as the sun sinks to relieve them of their blueblack treasures. At first, mama had a method of her own. Every night, she put out a net in the lagoon. Every morning she came bringing in a big basket full. One dawn, as she was untangling her catches' claws from the net, a man came up. He was dressed in boots, jeans, and a leather jacket. Mama thought he was another fisherman.

"What you got there?" he asked casually.

"Lobsters," answered mama. "Aren't they beauties?"

"Yes," said he. "Are those little ones good?"

"Oh, yes," said mama. "Best of all!"

"This one has eggs on it, doesn't it?" he asked.

"Is that what they are?" (From mama.)

"You shouldn't take those or the small ones," he said. "You're liable to deplete the stock of lobsters. One female lays 500,000 eggs sometimes, you know."

"Really," asked mama incredulously.

"The only time it's fair to take lobsters is during the months of the year that are spelled with an R. That excludes May, June, July, August."

"Ah," said mama sadly, always ready to sympathize with the underdog. "I'm sorry, you're certainly convincing. I'll have to put these back."

"Yes," said the man, "I'm glad I convinced you because" (and he showed his badge) "you see I'm the fish and game warden."

"Now it was mama's turn. "Ignorance is indeed bliss, isn't it?" she said.

That stopped our mama's lobstering until September, when she started again and in earnest. Once we gave lobsters as Christmas presents, tying bright bows and tiny silver bells around them and hanging them on friends' door knockers. We boiled them in sea water first. They turned a beautiful red.

Grunions are the most interesting fish in the world. When we found out about their love life, we felt sorry for them, but still ate them. They are like smelts, and about the same size. Their home is Southern California, too. It is interesting figuring out when they are going to run. We always wait for Alfred to tell us. No matter what the paper says, he never fails in his calculations. Grunions run during the high tides of the dark and the full of the moon. They come up on the beach just after the tide has turned. The female with millions of her sisters sweeps in to stand on her tail long enough to lay eggs in the sand. The male curls himself protectingly around her. Together they wriggle and twist back to the sea, and the eggs are washed into the ocean by the high tides two weeks later where they hatch into tiny fish.

Grunion-catching parties are fun. You build a fire on the beach and start waiting. Roasting ears of corn, wieners, and marshmallows keeps you from getting bored. Also you can't catch grunions without first singing, "Old Black Joe," "Carry me Back to Ol' Virginny," and "Good Night, Ladies."

Everyone has a different story to tell about his experiences but Hans Gude's is the funniest. He had always hooted at grunions. His cool Norwegian head had told him "Dey ver yust a mith." One hot summer's night he was persuaded to go fishing. He met his friends at the beach direct from his office. He wore business clothes. He and the others waited and waited. Finally the others gave up and went away. Hans stayed to enjoy the cool air. Tula was out of town. It was lonesome at home. He took off his shoes and socks, rolled up his trousers, and strolled down toward the water. He felt the sizzling surf around his ankles. He felt something else, too. "Grunions," he shouted. "Why bless my soul, grunions!" No one was there to offer competition or congratulations. Hans went wild. With his bare hands he grabbed them up, stuffing them in his coat pockets, his pants pockets, his shoes, and his socks. He tore off his shirt, made a bag out of it by tying together tail and arms and filled it. Hans afterward said, "Dey ver laying eggs all over the place. In my hands, in my pockets, even in my hair!"

Alfred knows best how to cook them. "Grunions Mit Onions is my motto," he says as he dips the last egg and cracker-crumbed critter out of the hot grease and throws in a batch of onions.

CHAPTER 28

Daddy never lets us forget that we make a living beachcombing and that we must continually turn barnacles into bread and butter, or in one way or another make our occupations count.

Daddy has trained us to keep a weather eye out for unusual objects on the beach. Scanning is part of our before breakfast exercises. The funniest thing daddy ever found was a dressmaker's form. He and mama almost came to blows when daddy brought the awful old rusted thing home. He simply wouldn't throw it back into the sea.

Daddy did different things at different times with the dummy. Once he made a model for a Woman's Club style show in Hollywood. She had a sail canvas head, with pink shell eyelids, and dark brown fishnet eyelashes. She had long braids of yellow fish net. She had a fish net stocking cap on her head. (It turned out to be so cute that daddy made Flo and me one.) She was elaborate with a shell covered bodice and full fish net skirt. We all loved her and were sorry to take her apart when the show was over.

Next, daddy made a ship's figurehead out of the "form." That was the best because Franz Bras, our artist, carved a beautiful wooden head for it, and painted it just enough to make it look as though the paint was coming off instead of being put on. Subsequently daddy made various things from his "form," never selling it, only renting it. At this particular moment it stands made into the silliest looking beachcomber you've ever seen. I suppose you'd call him a bar. He holds a tray full of glasses and from his ragged pockets peak bottles of champagne.

He's to be used by Mr. Errington for the Beachcomber Club at their annual Bel Air Bay club party.

The nicest thing I ever found on the beach was the "King." He is an Hawaiian swimmer. He has a magnificent physique but is blind. Bing Crosby brought him over for his picture, "Song of the Islands." Now he sings in a night club and looks very lonely.

Last summer he made the swim from Catalina Island to the mainland, a distance of 22 miles, in icy cold water. All day we heard reports on his progress. He was doing fine, he was still holding out, he would probably make it, and so on.

It was during the time of moonless nights. The earth and sea were dark as soon as the sunset. I sat watching, straining my eyes for the first sight of movement, my ears for the first faint splash of a weary arm. My heart was pounding mightily as I though of the blind Hawaiian, so far away from his homeland, attempting the almost impossible, so he could get publicity and attract greater crowds to the night club where he sang. It seemed sad, and I wondered what he was thinking, out there in the cold, black water. I longed to comfort him, somehow, to show my sympathy and friendship.

Suddenly and with hardly any noise, the King pulled himself out of the waters and slid panting to my side. His face and body were covered with heavy black grease. His breath was coming in great racking gasps. I put my arm around his shoulders, pressed my face close to his wet cheek for a moment, and said, "Oh, King, you made it, you made it!" He couldn't see, but I could. A quivering smile broke over his lips and I was thankful.

Careful watchers up and down the shore spotted the King and came running. An ambulance roared up and shouting crowds bore him away. I stood quite alone, by my little beacon fire, tears sprang to my eyes. In my hands was a greasy white bathing cap. The Hawaiian swimmer had made it! Yes, the King is the very nicest thing I ever found on the beach.

Another wonderful thing I found was Abraham. When we found him huddled on the rocks one cold rainy day, he was a sick, broken-winged pelican. In a few days he was practically running the place. We learned about pelicans from him. We netted anchovies for him to eat. He followed all of us around and like to have his back rubbed.

Daily his wild eyes grew more tender. He slept under my window on a barrel. Sometimes at night I awoke to find him staring in at me. I tapped gently on the glass and uttered clucking sounds. Abe then tied his neck into two or three knots, got in as uncomfortable a position as possible, and fell asleep.

One day Michael Miggins, a propman of M.G.M., told us he could use him in the movies if we would put him in a pen. We couldn't do that to Abe. Then he flew again. As he went soaring out to sea, we all ran excitedly to the shore, screaming "Abraham." He stayed out for an hour; then zoom! He came soaring in again. Oh, glorious! We had a friend who could fly. After that Abe came and went as he liked.

When we had guests and wanted to show off we stepped over to the sea, cupped our mouths with our hands, and called, "Abraham." More often than not a huge fluttering form picked itself up from the midst of squatting pelicans and gulls and flew to our sides. With loud squawks Abe gave greetings.

The last time we saw him, he came soaring in with a fish hook caught in his wing. We tried to untangle it but he wouldn't give us the time. He had business elsewhere. He flew off to sea with great flapping. Now all of us call "Abraham" every time we see pelicans but so far he hasn't answered. We miss him greatly. Still, it's some consolation to know that somewhere, one wild thing has felt the touch of a human hand and still remains free, but please, if you ever see a pelican who answers to the name of Abraham, notify us, won't you?

I believe of all the things daddy has ever made, I liked the whale-bone table the best. We found the fan-shaped collar bone on the beach at Portuguese Bend, which was once a whaling center. It took much lugging and stopping to get it home as whales are large, you know!

Daddy tried all kinds of experiments with it. Somehow, none of them did anything for it. It was still a whale bone. Daddy thought and thought. Ah, yes, he takes his slogan, "Beachcombing an art," seriously.

One evening we were entertaining friends at dinner. Among them was Erik Bolin, the decorator. To mama's surprise, as she greeted her guests, she saw looming from a corner the whale bone. It had become a table, holding cigarettes, magazines, and ash trays.

It was mounted on a pirate's chest, from whose side spilled shell beads, pearl beads, diamonds and rubies and a secret door slid back to reveal the same inside, with colored fish floats, the whole lighted with a soft undersea green light. "Out of this world," was Mr. Bolin's opinion. Daddy suggested that he could bring it to him the next day, but Mr. Bolin wanted to take it with him in his convertible. You could hardly see Mr. Bolin behind the steering wheel for the whale bone. Daddy stood looking after him as he drove away. He said ruminatively, "I wonder if the jewels could have had anything to do with his liking the table so well."

"Why?" questioned mama.

"His father was the court jeweler to the Czar of Russia, you know."

"Ah, I see," answered mama pointedly. Sometimes daddy has almost a sixth sense about selling.

We have good friends who are fishermen. They give us beautiful brown net and white corks which they can't use. None of them will take pay, although they always seem glad to get the lamps, net table cloths, coasters, and cork-bottomed goblets which we give them. Our west coast fishermen are not "lowly folk" at all. Some of them verge on big business. Most of them are Italian, Yugoslav, or Japanese nationality, and can usually swear in a number of different languages. They are friendly, love to give, and drink home-made wine.

Our friend Mr. Dick De Polo of Monterey has a purse seiner. His is a fine, large boat. He invited us to cruise with him for a week up around Seattle. We accepted, having visions of storms at sea, whales, and high adventure. None of these things materialized. We had delicious food and even luxury, not at all what we expected from a voyage on a fishing boat. Daddy, however, got an idea on the trip. It came about in this way. One day, when the sun was shining brightly and a million diamonds danced on the surface of the blue water, the *Walderon* rose and fell as she slid along over the kelp filled swells. One of the men sighted an object to starboard. "Cap," he shouted to daddy, "look! A treasure chest!" The fishermen loved to "kid" Eli about his beachcombing and never tired of getting daddy excited over imaginary jetsam which they conjured up. Daddy had a good laugh at his own expense and called for the binoculars. He looked through them a long time. "By Jove," he said, "that does look like a treasure chest." Mr. De Polo ordered the Skipper to put about, and away we went after what we all fest sure would turn out to be a packing box. As we neared it we saw first, an old iron chain, then an old iron lock, and finally were able to see the faint outline of an old green box. Daddy nearly died with excitement. The men pulled it up with their big hooks. As it came up over the side of the ship you could almost see jewels and laces spilling from its battered bulk. There it was on deck at last, a real honest-to-goodness treasure chest. Daddy worked on it all day rubbing its wood gently and lovingly. It was turning into a beautiful relic already, when daddy found a secret compartment and went wild again. He was rubbing the inside of the lid when suddenly a little sliding door sprang open as noiselessly and easily as if it had been oiled every day for years. This was something that happened once in a life time to a beachcomber. Daddy knew he'd been living right then.

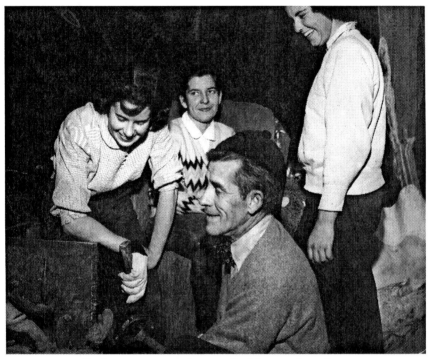

Finding a treasure chest set Daddy to making them.

Of course, finding the treasure chest set daddy making them. He made big ones, little ones, cigarette box ones, jewel box ones, and the ones he made looked older than the real one.

We all laughed one day when the Columbia set man picked up a chest daddy had made the day before, instead of the real one, because as he said, "This picture calls for a *really* ancient chest!"

CHAPTER 29

When Columbia pictures decided to use our house as background for Johnny Weismuller's series of pictures entitled "Jungle Jim's Adventures," the weather became the most important thing. All else paled before the momentous, gigantic question, "What is the visualization now?" The telephone rang every fifteen minutes the day before they began shooting. Mr. Fisher of "location" wanted to know about the weather. When darkness fell, he ceased calling.

Mama had been told there was to be a trained bird in the story, and that our dory door and pivot window were to be featured. She was delighted, dreamily contemplating a sweet white dove flitting about. She was disappointed, however, when the company arrived, to find that the bird was a crow and that our boat door was to be the entrance to a jungle saloon. However, she forgot her chagrin in the excitement and complete mad housishness of Columbia's making a "B." We never before had so much fun and got paid for it. At eight o'clock in the morning, busses, trailers, trucks, cameras, power machines, leading men, leading ladies, technicians, makeup men, script writers, heavies, Hawaiians, champion swimmers, directors, assistant directors, set men, grip men, caterers, a dog, a crow, and Johnny Weissmuller poured down the hill, and into Trade Winds Cove.

Daddy and I were having breakfast when a Hindu (Paul Marion of the Bronx), if you please, and four tough, tattered sailors (heavies, not villains), I'll have you know, dashed in the front door. "Hi," we said. "Hi," answered they. They were so jolly and loved to talk, which they did, as fast as they could right up to the minute they heard the director's whistle, whereupon they wiped the smiles off their faces, frowned wickedly and stormed out to face the cameras. Rube Schaeffer (the nicest heavy I've ever known) loved old things. He prowled around the house trying to spot the antiques between scenes. When he heard the director's signal, he quickly replaced an old lamp or mustache cup which he had been admiring, dashed to the door, squirmed in line with the rest and stalked out trying to look as mean as the bad man he was supposed to be. He nearly got left every time.

Johnny Weissmuller is a good swimmer despite a bit of a stomach. He has a suave haircut now, since his is no longer Tarzan. Blondie and Dagwood's dog acted in the picture with him. He is a darling, with one ear that falls down. Johnny said, "I can't miss in this picture, with two animals supporting me. This time I'll knock 'em dead."

This motley throng of delightful, zany people poured down the hill for four days, and we all became bosom friends. It was like a picnic all of the time. The caterers asked us to lunch, the Hawaiians entertained us with singing and dancing, and the divers brought us abalones and lobsters. The director said, "Hey, fellas, stop having so much fun and try acting a while."

Mama was careful to lock the back door when the Columbians were here. The reason for that was because she didn't want any one to come in the kitchen. Try as we will to keep that room straight, we can't. It always looks as though it's been stirred gently with a big spoon. Mama was at the sink trying to lessen the pile of dishes that seem to live on our drain board when to her utter dismay, Weismuller dashed in, grabbed our camping pan (the one with the smoked bottom), filled it with water, dashed out, threw the water on himself, dashed in again, hung the blackened pan back on the wall, yelled "Thank you," and dashed out again to play the part of a damp adventurer as the cameras whirred. Mama stood in the middle of the kitchen with a red, red face. She philosophized a bit. "Perhaps it's best not to try to hide anything." "Pride goeth before a fall," and "Who in the heck left the kitchen door unlocked?"

When we saw the picture at the neighborhood theatre, it made us feel sad to see Rube die so many times. He died out at sea, he died on the hill path back of our house, and died again coming through the boat oar gate. I guess we wouldn't have noticed that it was our Rube dying all over the place if we hadn't liked him so much. Columbia should be more careful and not overwork its heavies like that.

CHAPTER 30

The most fun we have is going on trips for driftwood. Since we've cleaned the beaches from San Simeon in the north to our own in the south we go to Oregon and Washington and sometimes Mexico. Daddy says "Go" is our middle name. We have all reached the status of true vagabondism. We can feel at home anywhere. We go in our station wagon, taking a big trailer for carrying our beachcombings and sleeping bags. We take wool blankets, seven spoons, seven plates, seven cups, seven breakfast food bowls (somebody might happen to drop in), a big knife, a little knife, a can opener, an iron pot, an iron skillet, and a big coffee pot. Anything else on a trip is too much. The last time we went to Oregon we wore jeans and wool shirts. It took us ages to get there as we immediately started seeing things other people never see on a trip, like the old Irishman who sang bits from operas and collected lame dogs. One, without a leg, walked on a little wooden peg, which his master had hewn for him. And, too, daddy has a side road complex, really a fixation. He simply cannot pass a side road without turning onto it. It's awful! All of a sudden daddy pulls over to he right. We go joggety jog down a dirt road for miles, expecting something all the time, none of us ever know for sure what. Mama says it's probably something in daddy's childhood that makes him do that. Sometimes we have to turn around and come back but sometimes the side road brings results and we find a place like we found the second night out. Tall, slim redwood trees stood proudly. A lopsided moon played peek-a-boo behind drifting clouds. A stream gurgled in places, kept deeply quiet in others. We crawled into our sleeping bags around a big fire and were sung to sleep by the creaking of frogs.

In the morning, Bungy was the first awake. She replenished the fire and started breakfast. Mama, lying in her sleeping bag, reveling in being on the road again (she's a hoboess), said sleepily, "If anyone ever tells me the woods are quiet, I'll know they've never been there. I never heard so much noise, frogs croaking, trees swishing, bugs gossiping."

"Oh, you know what that is," said Ba, "that's the loudness of the quietness." It was cold. Daddy handed Bungy his clothes to hang by the fire. He slipped into his warmish pants just as mama ventured bravely onto a log that had fallen and was forming a bridge across the creek. She was singing, "Oh, What a Beautiful Morn –" but the last syllable was drowned out by gurgles as mama slipped and went plop into the icy waters. Daddy nonchalantly shed his warmish pants and dived in after her. You think daddy doesn't love mama? The two of them swam around having so much fun that one by one we all deluged – that was our first bath on the trip.

Oregon was all yellow daisies, Christmas trees, sheep grazing on the hillside, blackberries growing beside the road, and blueberries. Mama was glad to see her old friend the huckleberry, spelled whortleberry, which she hadn't seen since her Oklahoma childhood days when she ate them off bushes which grew behind the little red school house.

We got our driftwood on Heceta Beach. It was foggy and blowing a thirty-mile gale, the morning daddy chose to get it. This beach is a sand-duney one and the sand is packed so hard that a

139

car can drive right along the water's edge. It was fun getting lost amid the dunes and hallooing for each other. The driftwood there is beautiful. Afterwards we camped in the forest. This time we picked our place systematically and got settled before dark. There's nothing comparable to camping in a forest. We're never afraid, no matter how deep into its impenetrableness we go. That's because our grandfather Reed told us one time, "There's never any reason for fear in the woods; caution, yes, but not fear. Tread lightly here, my little ones, so that you do not disturb even a skein of a spider web. Here, you find no maliciousness, no human hatred – only an instinct for protection. Take heed that you do not frighten these forest folk and you'll be safe as a bird in her nest." We've never forgotten what he said.

We went to sleep that night with bushy tops of tall straight pines rolling like waves far above our heads in the wind. "Like an evergreen sea," sputtered mama, her mouth full of huckleberries.

In the morning, a twisty piece of oak, covered with light green deer moss, acted as a centerpiece on the breakfast table, blackberries lay cradled in fern leaves in a basket. We had blueberry and pecan pancakes. Try them sometime, dee-licious, even without the Oregon setting.

Then mama went into the depths of green and took a bath in a crystal clear stream. She hung the towel and wash rag on a fir tree. She placed the soap on a bit of moss at her feet. She stood on pine needles. All this definitely went to her head. She acted as if she'd had champagne. She danced in and out among the trees singing over and over, "I had a bath in the forest!"

Afterwards we drove hard to reach San Francisco and the Emporium where daddy sold the load of driftwood. It's the nicest thing to deal in beachcombing. People ask questions about it, and you get so many new friends that way. "What are you going to do with it?" "Isn't it beautiful?" "This looks like a deer's head or is it a giraffe?" "Smells just like the sea, don't it?" "Makes me homesick!" Those are some of the remarks we hear.

We stopped at the St. Francis that night. "From forest to Francis," Flo Ann remarked cleverly.

When we reached our room in the hotel, mama threw herself on the bed and laughed until the tears rolled down her cheeks. "What's the matter?" we all demanded. "I don't know," she answered between giggles. "Somehow we look like so many as we gather around waiting to be assigned rooms. It always looks as though we've picked up one or two extra. Daddy and his deals. Always it's the same – Always he calls for two rooms with two double beds and one bath, then he turns to us and says, "You don't need a bath, do you?" I wonder what the clerk would have done if I had said, "Ah, no. I had a bath in the forest this morning with a pine tree tickling me behind and a huckleberry bush tempting me in front. A woodpecker knocked on the tree to my right while a ground squirrel ran along the log to my left." Sometimes mama surprises me!

We stopped at lovely Monterey coming back. This town used to have color without any paint. Now it has paint but not much color.

CHAPTER 31

Then there are our trips to Mexico. We start enjoying them when we stop on our way, at Phoenix, Arizona, to visit Dr. Harber. He has a big house and swimming pool and used to be mayor of Seminole, Oklahoma.

We think he's grand because he knows how to use money. One day while we were living in Seminole, he telephoned daddy to ask him to come by his office for an important conference.

Daddy was "needles and pins" to find out what he wanted to see him about, having visions of being appointed chief of something or other. He hastened to the mayor's office only to find out that Dr. Harber wanted to consult with him about his college curriculum. He was going back to school to daddy's alma mater, Oklahoma University. He was over sixty years old. The mayor made good grades in college in everything but business economics. He flunked that course. But he didn't care because he already had a million dollars which he had made in the oil business.

The last time we went to Guaymas Bay, Mexico, we had a hard time getting into the country and a harder time getting out. Getting in was hard because mama lost one section of her passport which she'd got at Nogales, Arizona, from the Spanish Consul … Five of us handed over three sections each of visa to a handsome, dignified officer behind a big, brown desk. Mama handed him two. He took them, began to count them off into six separate piles. "Uno, dos, tres; uno dos tres; uno dos, tres; uno, dos, tres; uno, dos, tres; uno, dos,-?" He looked blank, then slightly shocked. Mama broke in with, "Yo lost el visa de mi." The officer shrugged his shoulders, patiently and softly began counting again, "Uno, dos, tres; uno, dos, tres; uno, dos, tres; uno, dos, tres; uno, dos, tres; uno dos, -?" He looked at daddy, threw up both hands. Daddy looked at him and threw up both hands, too. The officer, with a deep sigh, began again, "Uno, dos, tres; uno, dos-?" A less dignified but no whit less handsome officer stood looking on sympathetically. He offered our officer a drink from his bottle of beer. Our man indignantly and self-righteously refused, "No, Pancho, no," before he started counting all over again. "Uno, dos, tres" –

We were ready to give up when another officer (oh, yes, handsome, too) came to our rescue. Casually, he opened a drawer, pulled out a form, wrote on it, and beckoned to mama to sign. She did. At last we were legally in Mexico.

We drove 420 kilometers to Guaymas Bay. We made camp in the late evening on a little point jutting into the bay off Miramar beach. Clouds hung low, waiting to play their part in the inspiring drama called simply "Sunset." Jagged peaks of hills encircling the bay stood waiting, too. Suddenly the play began. Infinity broke into a soft blaze of deepest red. Clouds became fluffy pink dreams, the hills became purple "fortresses, strong towers" to lean upon. The water showed green, blue, mauve, blue, green. Fish spring up, their silver bodies writhing ecstatically. A delicate rainbow formed itself into a sweet promise. Time stopped. Beauty hung breathless in space. Surely, there would never again be aught but this glory.

No word need be spoken at a time like this, but heart always says much to heart. An old man was standing ankle deep in water.

A battered straw hat was on his head. He held a shovel which he had been using to make a little dam to ward off the rising tide and keep it from surrounding his bamboo, palm-thatched shack. He was looking up, but when I turned he peered deeply into my eyes and smiled. We never spoke to each other but we became good friends all the same.

Daddy says anything can happen in Mexico. Everything usually does. In the morning we met Senor Carlos Morales Felgueres who was on business in Guaymas from Mexico City. He was so sincere in his apologies for being connected with anything so drab as accounting that we finally forgave him. Also he was sooo handsome and gallant. When daddy said, "good-morning, sir," he replied, "Senor, let me say that I was hungry and I was thirsty. Now, since you have spoken, I am filled, and my thirst is quenched." You could see him sweeping his plumed sombrero to the ground, although he had on bathing trunks and no hat at all.

All of us sat together on the shores of beautiful Guaymas Bay, talking about literature, music, and politics. He was better informed about our country than we were about his. He was intensely interested in who was to be our next President. Sometime during the morning the idea of breakfast seemed a good one. We strolled leisurely over to the pavilion where a string orchestra had started playing, and picked a table as close to the leaping fish as possible. The waters of Guaymas Bay lapped the sand under our table. Our waiter was sorry, no breakfast, but plenty of coca colas and beer. We girls and mama took coca colas. Senor Morales and daddy took beer. After a few apiece of each, Senor Morales decided to introduce daddy to

144

the joys of tequila. After several rounds of this drink, topped with lemon juice and salt chaser, and more coca colas for us girls, Senor Morales had an idea. We'd breakfast on crabs. It was simple. He'd order the waiters to dive in and spear us some. No sooner said than done. He did order them to and they did dive in.

To our utter amazement, Senor Morales rose from the table, excused himself in a formal manner, and dived in, too. It wasn't long until our table top was crawling with busy, jolly crabs, which the waiters and Senor Morales kept bringing on the ends of spears and dumping, before they fled laughingly and drippingly back into the waters of the bay for more.

What a breakfast that turned out to be, what with the boiling of the poor little crabs and Senor Morales cracking their claws with a beer bottle with as much dignity as a judge pounding his gavel. We washed the crab meat down with coca colas, tequila, and beer respectively.

We had barely finished eating, when the proprietor of the pavilion, Senor Armando Valverdo, came over, bowed low and invited us to his barbecued turtle feast that afternoon. If we cared to, we could see the meat being prepared now. Daddy, before we could audibly demur, accepted, and asked if he could have the shell, too. When we arrived at the pit, the cooks were pounding the turtle to death before dipping the flesh in sauce and cooking it over an open fire. It was huge, two yards across.

At this point mama said she thought it was definitely time for everyone to go swimming, which we did, mama in her black Spanish skirt and bright red tee shirt. Women in Guaymas do not wear slacks or bathing suits. Only tourists do and over mama's dead body is she going to be mistaken for a tourist.

Daddy's eyes nearly popped out of his head when he saw mama walking calmly into the water with two other women fully clad. When they came out they all sat on the beach in the sun to dry. You needn't say that mama can't see the other person's point of view.

After we'd lunched on barbecued turtle (it came out sort of green on top, then sort of black, then sort of white), Senor Morales invited us to dine with him at his hotel while Senor Valverdo invited us to sleep that night under his palm shed. Daddy carried the turtle shell with trailing entrails still clinging to it and dumped it into the shallow side of the bay. He hoped it would be clean by morning.

Dinner was nine o'clock and seven courses long. It included three kinds of fish and mangoes. Afterwards we went to La Plaza and danced until four o'clock in the morning. The Ba and Bungy slept in the car.

For a week afterwards every time we thought of that day, we turned sort of green, but now when we think of it we have only happiness, but you simply can't mention beer and tequila to daddy.

The next day, we found Johnny and got on with our business of beachcombing. He took us rummaging in his 16-foot motor boat with a dinghy attached. We roamed around the coast, until we came to a spot where Johnny thought there were shells. He cast anchor. We swam ashore. Johnny caught totoaba and Boca Dulce. We fried them over an open fire and ate them with tortillas. We found millions of shells.

"Adios amigo" are the saddest words in the world, and we always put them off as long as possible in Mexico. It's awful leaving our good, good friends. When we got back to the border, a sandy-haired, bespectacled, stern-visaged American officer saw no earthly reason for daddy to come into Arizona with a foul-smelling turtle shell. Daddy was the most insulted I've ever seen him. There was more to the turtle than met the eye. A symbol of friendship could not be left behind. He went slightly berserk declaring that he would sit right there with his turtle until he could get somebody to say he could bring it across.

Mama was disgusted, but after seeing that "look in daddy's eye" said, "Come on, girls, we might as well go see what we can do." We left daddy in Mexico sitting dejectedly nursing his big green turtle shell. It was frightfully embarrassing. It took the banker, the mayor, and a lawyer to get daddy across the border with his turtle. The officer never did quite understand that daddy was going to make a lamp out of it.

Today, old turtle clings to a piece of silver driftwood, hung on the walls of Kelbo's Hawaiian Barbecue in Hollywood. Green ivy and philodendron spill decoratively from its sides, while behind it burns a soft, rosy light.

CHAPTER 32

Then daddy decided to go to Oklahoma beachcombing for popcorn peppers. He got the idea when Uncle Tom sent us one for Christmas. It was red and old-fashioned. When daddy wrote to him asking if they could be bough in gross lots Uncle Tom replied he thought so and for ten cents apiece. Daddy intended making them into canapé trays and cigarette holders.

We went by train because none of us had ever been on one. It was fun sleeping in a berth. Daddy reserved three lower ones all in a row. We giggled so much when we went to bed that mama was afraid we'd be put off the train at some station or other, and there were a few where we didn't care to have his happen to us. So many villages through the country brought us only impressions of drabness and runny-nosed children as we looked out the windows when the train made a brief pause. It was good though to see some of ht rest of America and to realize that here in these desolate area where human beings were huddled together, went on the same drama of birth and death and "in between" as went on it – well – say, Hollywood, and that these people were as important as the geniuses of the world in – well – say electing a President.

When we reached Oklahoma we were surprised. There were two things which impressed us during our stay there. Abundance and the "do or die" spirit. Fore'n'aft, starboard, and port, there is an abundance of everything in this state and there's a look on everyone's face which says plainly, "Ah, I'll never give up."

We'd heard about Okies from John Steinbeck, whose writings we like no end, so were shocked when Mr. H. W. McNeill met us at the station in Oklahoma City in a new Cadillac with a chauffeur. From then on our stay was one whirl of luxurious festivity. Our eyes, which were used to simple beach fare, nearly popped out of our heads at the elaborate boards prepared by our "do or die" hosts and hostesses.

We stayed at the Oklahoma Club and were waited on hand and foot by Negro boys. We were entertained royally by the Dixon Grissos in their charming Nichol's Hill house and gorged ourselves with black Lilly's Louisiana cooking.

We were taken by the Capital without a dome and the Governor's mansion surrounded by oil wells. Mama told us about the time she and a few other members of The League of Women's Voters had been guests at dinner there while Bill Murray was governor. She said there were tall glasses of spring green onions on either end of the table and Bill took a chew of tobacco when everyone else lighted a cigarette after dessert. He commanded respect, however, as he kowtowed to one and knew the Oklahoma Constitution forwards and backwards, and no wonder as he himself had written it when Indian Territory became a state.

We reached Seminole in late November via Clark Craig's home in Shawnee. Things started there when Clark gave a Neanderthal party for Bonnie his wife on their anniversary. Everyone came dressed as a cave man or woman. Fur skins, hair and leaves were the favorite costumes. Dinner was served around a low table, while guests sat on animal skins on the floor. Dinosaurs stood about the room amidst thick foliage, and everyone had a big T-bone steak, with all the fix'ns, topped off with Neanderthal ice cream men with whipped cream hair and a huge three-layer cake with a stone age village on top made out of icing.

It was cold enough to "freeze the horns off a muley cow" when we hit Seminole and were whisked from one party to another, we children in high glee. We remember Doc and Verna's house built like a Taos, New Mexico, pueblo with beautiful hand-made furniture covered with deer hide. We also remember the huge silver bowl full of black walnut halves, salted and roasted, the first we'd ever tasted. Doc's real name was Doctor Claude Chambers and he had officiated at Bungy's birth. He was a regent on the board of directors of the University of Oklahoma and a full-blooded Cherokee Indian. He also had a buffalo farm.

Daddy let us go everywhere with mama and him until James T. Jackson and Sadie gave their party. But after that he said he thought he'd better draw the line somewhere. It was all right for James T. to hang from the crystal chandelier in his ballroom shouting, "I'm Tarzan," but when he got into an argument with the editor of the opposing newspaper and started breaking Sadie's classical records over the editor's head that was carrying things a bit too far, even if he was the smartest man in town.

We were allowed to go to Elmer and Mauda Harber's skating party at their hunting lodge on the shores of Lake Wewoka but were not allowed to stay for the hoedown music of the "Catfish String Band." Everyone else had a "rip roarin'" time. Daddy said he nearly split his sides laughing at Elmer's stories during dinner.

Elmer always stopped before the punch line, pushed a bunch of peas onto his knife with his fork, and neatly popped them into his mouth without losing one. Some folks in Oklahoma used their knives as much as the British but not in altogether the same way. Elmer and Mauda seemed important to us because mama told us about the time they had redecorated a bedroom and put in a new bathroom in their beautiful Colonial house a few miles from town. They did this for their honored guest, Mrs. Eleanor Roosevelt, when she was in town giving a speech to the Camp Fire girls. They did the rooms in the President's wife's favorite color, blue. Mama and daddy went to the luncheon Mauda gave for a "select few." They thought Mrs. Roosevelt was charming although her voice was a little high. They loved the way she wouldn't talk about Washington or politics. She only talked about Camp Fire girls. The dinner dance, attended by a "select many," was very gay. "Yippees" and "Whoopees" were frequent throughout the evening and Eleanor had a good time "by gum."

Oklahoma is a dry state, but there are many kinds of spirits there and not all of them just high either. The spirit we noticed most was the one of friendly helpfulness.

And there was Tulsa! Ah, Tulsa! Big houses crammed with period furniture, all periods; rich decorators; grandfathers with pleasant faces, silvery gray hair, and shiny nails done by their favorite manicurists that very morning; white shirts, black ties, and Brooks Brothers suits; Homburgs; *the* Country Club; gossip; corks popping; women in mink coats being put to bed at parties; the opera (Maud Lorton, owner of the *Tulsa World* is responsible for that); ballet, yes, ballet, where we sat way down in front in order that our friend, Mrs. Witcher, could introduce us to her friends, the ballet dancers with long Russian names. Afterwards they said, "Oh, how sweet you were to drive all the way from Oklahoma City just to see us!"

We were guests of George Norvell and Alberta Simpson Matteson but not at the same time. They had been Mr. and Mrs. Norvell when we lived in Seminole, but in Tulsa they had each married someone else.

Mrs. Matteson's grandfather, O. D. Strother, discovered the first oil well in Seminole. Everyone called him crazy O. D. because he kept spending all of his money buying up land. One of his lady friends (he had a good many) was a medium and told him that she had been told by her control that there was oil in those parts. He had a sign in his general store which read, HOG FEED AND COFFINS – HALF PRICE TO WIDOWS AND ORPHANS.

He died before his first oil well was "brought in." His last words were, "Here, take this hundred dollars. It's all I have in the world. Buy that east forty and tell them to drill deeper."

Because her grandfather was thought crazy and was really so smart Alberta was left quite "well off." Mrs. Matteson spends her money running around the world. Mama said Alberta was in so many different places in a year that she (mama) had to keep two address books just for her.

We liked Mr. Matteson, her husband. He was jolly and treated us to everything in sight, from banana splits to Indian costumes. He was handsome and looked exactly like a picture of an "old grad" – especially in his tails and white tie.

George Norvell's house was fun, too. His wife, Opal, had been his secretary. She was beautiful but also efficient. They had four children. That's what made their house so much fun. Mr. Norvell was a Juvenile Judge but daddy said at heart he was a song writer. He belonged to the Rotary Club Quartet in Seminole along with Bob Chase, Doc Chanbers, and Sam Hammond. Daddy said if George had worked as hard at publishing his songs as he worked at being a Judge, he might have had a number one hit on the juke boxes around over the country.

Ah, Tulsa; Cadillacs; real monkeys in cages shipped in from Africa for a party; the food coming from Antoine's in New Orleans; breakfasts for $100 a plate, and a hundred places to go every day; but we never did see any oil.

The morning our train sped West towards sunny California we were sad. On both sides of the track were thickets of black jack and dogwood, the little trees glittering now in the sunlight, their black arms blanketed with brittle ice. Snow covered the hills and cotton patches where brown pods held wisps of unpicked cotton, whose gray whiteness contrasted strangely with the white whiteness of the snow. Here and there red berries glowed brightly from their vines clinging to the tall sycamore trees and purple 'possum grapes hung temptingly above the reach of a boy or a girl or a cow. Bare trees held little orange persimmons heavy with the frost, which was busy converting their puckeriness into mushy sweetness. Big clumps of olive green mistletoe with clear tapioca-like berries served as windbreaks for squirrels in the maple trees. A de-shucked corn field looked yellow and happy but almost at once looked brown and sad as the sun passed behind a cloud and crows flew up here and there, cawing mournfully.

"Yep," we were "all fired" sorry to be a-leavin' Oklahoma.

CHAPTER 33

Walking on the beach is like walking in a garden. All around you is beauty. Sea weed cast up by the tide reveals every kind of vegetable, comparable to our own earth fruit. There are long green onions, bright red peppers, bunches of grapes. The fish have salad and fruit, too.

When I trudge the beach alone I like the feeling of being one with the rocks, the waves, and sky. I feel this way most on our "dream rock." It's reached walking on the sandbar, when the tide is still low enough to encircle gently its base and run off again. I climb to its top and lie down. The sun is warm, the air cool, the black stone damp. A gull flies above, the one living thing besides · me. I go to sleep. The tide creeps in. Suddenly, icy water splashes about me, on top of me, in my eyes, my mouth. I cling to the peak upon which I have been lying, while all around I can see only green water churning angrily.

I am fearful but I feel exultant at being so close to the sea's mystery; before I step calmly off my fortress and wade to shore in the receding tide! I recommend this for anyone with jaded nerves. Surely you can find you a rock somewhere!

Sometimes I think it would be better if we didn't have so many unexpected happenings in our lives. We could get things under better control. When I spoke to daddy about this he said earnestly, "The way to get around that is to expect the unexpected."

I give up! The nearest daddy ever came to a nervous breakdown was when he hired an efficiency expert to figure out how he could increase his volume, decrease his expenses, and thus increase his profit. The efficiency expert did have one, and the family (everyone but daddy) went to visit him in the hospital to apologize. Just the same daddy lays claim to the distinction of being the first beachcomber to make the Wall Street Journal and especially to forgetting which issue it was.

"How can you be efficient with a business whose stock is some flotsam, some jetsam?" he defends himself belligerently.

"Don't forget it consists of ideas unlimited and courage, not a little," says mama as she kisses daddy.

It's not so bad living around daddy after you catch on. For instance when daddy says energetically, "Let's get up early in the morning and start the ball rolling," we aren't surprised if we see him at nine-thirty still reading *Huckleberry Finn,* practicing his tumbling on the bed, or leaning back against piles of pillows studying all the verses of "The Star Spangled Banner," which he's never known and has sworn to master.

We know when daddy says, "We're going south to Mexico tomorrow for shells and driftwood," that we're just as likely to go north to Eureka, so we pack sweaters just in case. You see it's really easy . . . !

Mama turns housekeeping off and on like a water faucet. Some mornings she rises early and tears into being a good wife and mother exactly like she's acting the part on a stage. Other days she's a gypsy and you can't do anything about it. Poor mama, the best she can possibly achieve, even when she gives it her all, is a sort of orderly disorder! Meals at our house, however, are always fun.

Mama and daddy always manage somehow to have them gay, gala affairs. Now since we children are older, we appreciate this. We know it hasn't been so easy for mama to make happy conversation while daddy smilingly measured sparse helpings, praying the "main dish" would reach around.

Mama and daddy have their points. I've given the matter earnest consideration and I wouldn't change them, even if I could.

And so happy days catapult themselves one after another like music pouring from a scale played on a piano. This water and this beach may keep us busy for a long, long, time, and yet I can't help wondering.

Last Christmas we had a dinner party. Everyone came despite the heavy California mist. We ate outside by the big fireplace. We placed lighted candles between the big rocks that form the mantle and all over the hills on both sides. Colored lights brightened the royal palms. A long driftwood table was covered with white net, dotted with silver and gold star-fishes. A polished baleen from a whale in the center held pineapples, avocados, and English walnuts. Dessert was served on black-lipped Tahitian pearl shells. The sea wore a gray-green dress with a girdle of purple. The moist cypress trees gave generously of their fragrance. Everyone had an awfully good time. Mama and daddy beamed. At ten o'clock we walked to the gate with our last departing guest.

Daddy adjusted the private property sign. I thought to myself, everyone's private property is an acre of sunshine, a field of stars, and the path the moon makes upon the waters. I was glad for this as we trudged arm in arm to the house. Flo stirred the fire and daddy went to the kitchen, "You know, I always say turkey and dressing are better cold," he managed from a mouthful of them. Mama ate a salted nut. Then Ba put on her new ballet slippers and drew herself into a cozy corner of the steps by the fireplace. Bungy tried on her skates again. Flo yawned while I hummed a last carol. At ten-thirty the clock struck three. We were used to that. Daddy joined us and broke into our reveries. "Did you notice how many people said, "Eli, I guess you're settled for life?"

"Yes," said mama. "I wonder what settled for life really means?"

"I wonder, too," said daddy. "Sounds sort of final, doesn't it, sort of like it's all over." He dreamed fire dreams for a while, then went on. "You know, I was reading the other day about Grugsholm

159

Castle. It has eighteen rooms and is for sale for five hundred dollars – oh, yes, it has a bathroom, too, and is where the Earl of Bothwell was imprisoned. I wonder how beachcombing is in Denmark?

"How utterly fantastic!" said mama. She was busily toasting marshmallows; the heavenly satisfaction look was on her face.

Printed in the United States
58900LVS00002B/502-624